CURRENTS IN THE STREAM

Miramichi People and Places

D1216571

WAYNE CURTIS

Published by Gooselane Editions Ltd., 248 Brunswick Street, Fredericton, New Brunswick, Canada, E3B 1G9

Acknowledgements

I would like to thank the following people who have helped me in writing these chapters: Sherie Anderson, John Boise, Belva Brown, Cathy Bryan, John Burchill, Carl Burns, Susan Butler, John Curtis, Earl English, Fred Farrell, James Fraser, Marvin Flemming, Graham Galloway, Marguerite Jardine, Edith McAllister, James MacRae, John McKay, Warren MacKinley, Rev. Mersereau, Wendy Robb, Peter Snowball, Doug Shanahan, Glenna Taylor, Doug Underhill, Jack Ullock, and Theodore Walls.

Without the help of Doug Underhill, Earl English and James Fraser, in particular, this book would not have been possible.

Book design by Sabine Campbell
Cover photograph by Ferris
Typesetting by Folster & Cummings

Canadian Cataloguing in Publication Data.
Curtis, Wayne, 1945-

Currents in the Stream

ISBN 0-86492-092-X.

1. Miramichi River Valley (N.B.) — History. 2. Miramichi River Valley (N.B.) — Biography. I. Title.

FC2495.M5C87 1988   971.5'21   C88-098598-4

F1044.M5C87 1988

I dedicate this book to my wife Janet and to my sons Jeff, Jason and Steven.

Contents

Illustrations

Foreword

Away back in 1977 I marked, corrected, and proof-read submissions to a newspaper programme called *Write-On*. Consistently excellent articles came from a person who signed his name Wayne Curtis. Later, to my great joy, the individual who attended my university classes from 1984 to 1987, the one who always contributed the most carefully researched essays, proved to be the same person.

Wayne visited my high school classes at James M. Hill in Chatham and read a number of his short stories. This left a lasting impression on the students and many commented upon his "close to the soil" material, asking me if "good authors always write autobiographically." Wayne has always been interested in people, as his many articles show, and in this book he writes about seemingly ordinary individuals with special skills, like John Brophy, the expert canoist, and the guides of Charlie Wade, as well as the strange ghost of the Dungarvon Whooper and such widely-known people as Lord Beaverbrook and Ted Williams the Baseball Hall-of-Famer. But Wayne writes about Williams the fly-fishermen and member of another Hall-of-Fame—that of Doaktown's Salmon Museum.

Wayne's short story, "In Keeping Our Best Traditions," expresses the values which he and his grandfather share when they allow two deer (a fawn and a doe) to pass by unhurt— "Not even for a winter's supply of meat could they kill"— while the hard work which is also part of the Curtis heritage is shown in "The Woodcutters," celebrating work, family ties, and the love of God in "a deep harmony that only we could feel."

Carl Burns

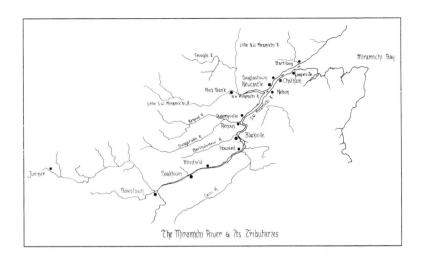

The Miramichi River & Its Tributaries

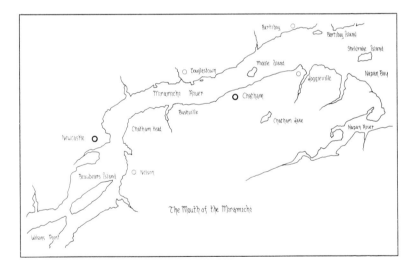

The Mouth of the Miramichi

INTRODUCTION

The Miramichi River winds its way northeast across the province of New Brunswick. Its headwaters are in the hills about seven miles upstream from the village of Juniper. Here the Little Southwest Branch of the main stem emerges from a series of springs and brooks, making a small stream that gradually increases in size until it's a full-sized river completing its journey some 150 miles downstream at Escuminac, flowing into the Atlantic Ocean.

Where the river begins in the hills above Juniper, there is a kind of divide. Here the river's altitude reaches its highest point above sea level. Beyond the divide the land slopes to the west with its streams flowing toward the Saint John River. Landmarks on the river above Juniper are places called Chickadee Hawk and Broken Toe. Such places would have been named by woodsmen after experiences in a certain section of the woods and used thereafter to help identify the area in lumbering circles.

Ten miles downstream from Juniper, the Little North Branch makes it confluence at the "forks" and from here down the much larger stream picks up tributaries such as McKeil Brook, Burnt Hill Brook, Rocky Brook, the Taxis River, Burnt Land Brook, Big Hole Brook, the Cains River, the Bartholomew River, Indian Town Brook, Elm Tree Brook, the Barnaby River, the Northwest Miramichi River (with its tributaries—the Little Southwest, and the Big and the Little Sevogle), the Bartibog River, Black Brook, the Napan River and the Tabusintac River. There are many other lesser tributaries in this drainage system, too many to mention.

The Miramichi winds through a remote wilderness with regions of heavy forest, abandoned farmlands, cultivation, lumbering communities, villages and towns. In the village of Juniper, during summer, a man can jump across the river with a canoe pole. The most downriver village on the river proper is Loggieville: here the river is one mile wide.

There are other communities below Loggieville: Napan, Bay Du Vin, Baie-Sainte-Anne and Escuminac on the south side and Burnt Church, Neguac and Tabusintac on the north.

These communities, however, are considered to be on Miramichi Bay and, this being a river book, are not mentioned here.

The major trading centres on the Miramichi are Newcastle and Chatham with approximately 6,000 people in each town and a drawing area of some 30,000. The attraction in these towns for industry is that they both have deep-water seaports, access to the Montreal/Moncton railway line, and commercial and military airports. These, and the continually advancing highway system with its new river bridge at Chatham and a proposed new bridge for Newcastle (to replace the existing Morrissy Bridge), encourage industrialists. The communities along the river have grown mainly because of the lumber industry. From the headwaters (heading northeast) they are: Juniper, Boiestown, Doaktown, Blackville, Renous, Millerton, Newcastle, Nelson, Douglastown, Chatham and Loggieville.

Every village on the river has a sawmill, with the larger centres having several lumber-related factories. Newcastle now has the world's largest pulp and coated-paper mill, Miramichi Pulp and Paper. But the Miramichi remains a one-major-resource river, depending on the lumber industry in one way or another for most of the employment. Other industries here are fishing, mining and tourism. While fishing has lessened and mining has all but disappeared in recent years, the tourism trade is growing through the government's encouragement of non-residents travelling to the Miramichi to vacation and fish for Atlantic salmon.

During the 1930s and '40s, many of the upriver reaches (above the tideway) were bought up by American sportsmen who built cabins and now spend their summers fly-fishing for the salmon. Large companies, such as the Colgate people, Reece Candy Company, Dupont, General Electric and Angelhart Industries have operated lodges on the river, employing guides, cooks and caretakers. A number of river people now depend upon these foreign-owned outfitters for seasonal employment.

The Miramichi has always been world-famous. It is rich in folklore and legend associated with the lumber woods, the stream drives, the shipbuilding and the Miramichi salmon. The river is somehow mystical and I suppose, when we depend so much on the natural resources of the region, mysticism becomes a part of our lifestyle. The Miramichi mysticism is difficult to explain to an outsider, but it is here. Perhaps the river people can see themselves as something different than what they really are, taking a spiritual concept over the material pleasures from which they are alienated for one reason or another. Characters seem to grow superlative here.

The Miramichi is also known as "mighty." This is an adjective associated wih the log drives, as in the old days it was a mighty hard stream to drive, especially in the wild reaches of the headwaters. The river remains mighty today. We are still known for having the best Atlantic salmon river in the world. We have an exciting history, a heritage of gallantry in the wilderness with colourful rough-and-ready adventurers and folk heroes who wrote their own songs, made their own entertainment, while raising large families in a frontier perhaps as rugged as any in the world. The legends are still here, exaggerated now by the distance in time and the magic of looking back. To be sure, the wilderness is still here as is the beautiful river. It's one that we've managed to keep so clean that we can drink its water, and of this we are mighty proud. We have kept our river pure when other countries, supposedly more sophisticated, have neglected theirs. We have watched some busier parts of this country develop into not-so-attractive places.

The Miramichi people are creative and resourceful. They are fun-loving and have a sense of humour. Some have an interest in the arts, with an appreciation for literature and music. Many can sing and dance or play an instrument of some kind; they pride themselves on a non-materialistic appreciation of the simpler things in life. Through the years, the river folk have written many of their own songs and we boast the longest consecutively running folksong festival in North America.

There are few class distinctions in Miramichi and most find that we are the same people "front and back." The Miramichier is an exaggerated Canadian; New Brunswick's New Brunswicker. Our houses are little white boxes on hillsides overlooking the river. There is a bond among us; we are held together through this remote section of Canada by a simple flow of water. Yet when it comes to individual characters we are all islands in the stream. I really came to appreciate the Miramichi bond when I set out to do research for this book. I got the same warm hospitality from Marvin Fleming and his wife in Juniper as I did from Matilda Murdock in Loggieville. Both had the teapot ready and some home-cooked chocolate cake; while Murdock was a champion fiddler, the Flemings were devoted square dancers.

For the size of our population and the "brain drain" caused by low employment levels, we have sent forth a good number of people to make their mark on the higher stages of the world.

We've had two Fathers of Confederation, and a cabinet minister in Great Britain; we've sent a lady to New York's Carnegie Hall; we've had a Miramichier in the Boston Symphony; we've had premiers, lieutenant-governors, senators and more than our share of fine writers including Monsignor Hickey of Chatham and David Adams Richards of Newcastle. We have a fine artist in Dr. Richard Howe. In fact, the Miramichi can boast more resource people per capita than most isolated regions. Perhaps this can be attributed to the fact that the atmosphere is soothing; it's a region of tranquillity. This combines with our legacy of mysticism, legend and hard times to nourish the creative mind. The aforementioned people came from poor backgrounds to make a success of themselves through their own resources.

And yet, I feel sometimes that our region has been neglected by governments. During the 1960s our university (St. Thomas) was moved from Chatham to Fredericton. Newcastle's Nurses' Training School was also moved away. CFB Chatham is said to be phasing out. The Miramichi/Nashwaak Railway has gone, as have a good number of the old ways of the river. Still we are advancing in a positive yet conservative manner: with an eye on a turbulent, exciting past and a cautiously optimistic eye to the future. We are a grass-roots people combining our human and natural resources. In this book I've written about only *some* of our people and places. The story of the Miramichi is very rich and varied and no doubt other Miramichiers would have made other selections. But I can't apologize for writing from my personal "slant" on the river and its people. I just hope that others will be encouraged to tell more. There's plenty more to tell.

It's been said that the Miramichi is not so much a geographic location as it is a state of mind. Alden Nowlan, the late Fredericton poet, once looked out across the river at Chatham and said to local writer Dave Butler, "You have a paradise here."

1
JUNIPER

The village of Juniper sits on the banks of the Little Southwest Branch of the mainstem Miramichi River about seven miles from the river's headwaters. This is a well-kept, nicely manicured lumbering community, nestled in a valley between the heavily forested summits of the province's extreme interior. From the highest hills overlooking the settlement one can see white-painted buildings clustered along a street. In the centre of the community there are a huge lumberyard and the sawmill, its refuse-burning teepee puffing smoke out over the town. The Miramichi River that winds through the settlement is, seen from the hilltop, just a scattered ribbon of jewels sparkling beneath the trees. Near the mill, the stream is partially dammed up to form a small deadwater for the mill's use. The rumble of the mill itself can be heard to the outermost edges of this tiny community. Along the street there are churches, schools, lodge hall, a modern post office, a false-fronted general store, legion hall, a cenotaph honouring the community's war dead and many beautiful contemporary homes.

Juniper can be reached by taking Highway #107 off Highway #8 at Nashwaak Bridge. A back highway, which is partially a dirt road, runs from Boiestown up the river through Parkers Ridge and Cross Creek. Another route cuts through the town of Bristol from the Saint John River.

The community (never officially incorporated) has grown around the Juniper Lumber Company's sawmill, the town's chief employer. Down the river at Juniper Station, there is a tree plantation which is operated by the Irving people. Almost every employed person in this settlement of 800 works in the lumber business on one end or the other.

The Moncton/Edmundston Railway Line (CNR) was built through this region in 1905, but Juniper was not founded until 1914 when two lumbermen, George Gilmore and George Foster, built a sawmill on the north bank of the river. It was said that the two men were portaging the portable mill into the hills above Juniper but got bogged down in mud while trying to ford the river. They assembled the mill on the riverbank here and began to saw lumber; the town grew around the mill. The Juniper Lumber Company mill stands in nearly the same location today.

In 1915, the sawmill was purchased by Flemming and Gibson Limited. This company was owned by the Hon. J.K. Flemming and Charles Rogers. In 1917, Mr. Samuel Billings became a partner to Flemming, buying out Rogers's interest. Mr. Billings came to Juniper that year and served the company as general manager until his retirement in 1957, when he moved to Woodstock.

But Mr. and Mrs. Walter Turnbull were said to be the first people to take up residence in Juniper. This was sometime just prior to Billings's arrival. Turnbull's grandson, Clarence Bell, was the first child born in Juniper.

The town was given its name for the many juniper trees that grow nearby. Juniper Brook, a Miramichi tributary that makes its confluence here, is an excellent trout stream. The south and north branches of the Miramichi River near the village abound with salmon and grilse.

The first schoolhouse in Juniper was built in 1923. Earl Gartley was appointed teacher. But it wasn't until 1938 that the community could support a church. That year, the Anglican and the Baptist faiths joined their efforts and constructed the new Union Church. Two years later, the Roman Catholics constructed their church as well as a priest's residence.

Through the years there have been many fires in Juniper. In 1924, the Juniper Mill burned to the ground. Losses were estimated at $30,000. In 1941, the blacksmith shop and a dry kiln shop were destroyed. The mill burned again in 1945 and this time almost the entire community was lost to the blaze. Other buildings destroyed in that fire were stores, post office, machine and blacksmith shop, planing mill, ladies' wear shop, garage and two dry kilns, as well as three private homes.

In 1925, J.K. Flemming was elected as a Conservative MP in the federal government. His sons, Hugh John and Weldon M. Flemming, along with Mr. Billings, carried on the business. Billings succeeded Mr. Flemming as company president. J.K. Flemming was re-elected in 1926, but took ill and died on February 10, 1927 at the age of 59.

J.K. Flemming's son, Hugh John, later went into politics and was elected as an MLA for Carleton County in 1944. In 1952, he became Premier of New Brunswick. By this time his brother Weldon had become general manager of the lumber company. It was said that their father was always thinking of benefits for the community and was an extremely generous man. He was instrumental in building Castle Hall, where the Knights of Pythias Lodge was instituted in 1924. This building also served as a Sunday School classroom and a hall for school concerts.

The tree plantation in Juniper Station was organized in 1958.

Juniper was hit by fire again in 1961, and this time a planing mill, dry kiln, garage and a dimension mill were destroyed. Restoration had just been completed when the mill burned again in 1964. Weldon Flemming sold out to Hugh John, who became president, with his head office in Fredericton. Flemming and Gibson and S.W. Bell of Stickney then joined forces, with Bell becoming general manager of both the Juniper and Stickney mills. The new mill (this one all-electric) opened for production in November 1964.

Samuel Billings died April 2nd, 1966 and Weldon Flemming died February 19th, 1967.

From 1971, Flemming and Gibson's mill was managed through the Dead River Lumber Company until 1974, when Hon. Hugh John Flemming retired as an MP in Ottawa and resumed management.

On April 22nd, 1977, Flemming and Gibson Limited was placed in receivership by the Imperial Bank of Commerce. The Juniper Lumber Company was incorporated in August 1977 and the mill began operating again that September.

On October 16, 1982, Hugh John Flemming died.

The economy in this river town remains stable and, like any community, its most important asset is its human resources. The people here are wholesome and beautiful in spirit.

2
BOIESTOWN

The quaint old village of Boiestown is nestled on the south side of the river near where Burnt Land Brook and the Taxis River make their confluence with the Miramichi River, some halfway between the town of Newcastle and the city of Fredericton (on Highway #8). This is the geographic centre of the province of New Brunswick, or: a tiny settlement that stands on the river flats, consisting of large wood-frame houses, general stores, inns and service stations in a row along the main street. This is the first river town on Highway #8 northeast of Fredericton.

Just northeast of the village are mills owned by the Ashley Colter Company, Tobique Lumber, and the Dead River Lumber Company. Nearby there are a ball park and fairgrounds as well as a take-out restaurant. Up the highway in the old part of town there are the post office, churches, schools, general stores, and fire and ambulance services (both volunteer). The Central New Brunswick Woodsmen's Museum is located between the mill and the old town, housing craft shops and banquet halls as well as the office of the Miramichi Salmon Association, a conservation group formed during the early 1950s to help protect the salmon resource.

This is one of the oldest villages in the northeast, founded in 1821 by a man who was said to have had "considerable wealth and a strong back and mind," and whose accomplishments would later inspire the villagers to name the town Boiestown in his honour. He was Thomas Boies, an American from Bedford, New Hampshire.

When Boies arrived on the Miramichi River in the summer of 1821, he was 32. He had been born in Bedford in September of 1789, one of a family of ten children. His father, John Boies, was a soldier who had participated in the battles of Hubbard-ton and Stillwater and had been wounded in the arm. He had suffered with Washington's army at Valley Forge in the winter of 1777-78, and had marched with John Sullivan's army, gain-ing a wealth of military experience before settling in Bedford. Later, the Boies family moved to Maine where John became a farmer and a trader, eventually dying there; he was buried at Skowhegan.

A decade after Thomas Boies arrived on the Miramichi River, Robert Cooney wrote the following account of the village Boies had established:

> Here at the mouth of the Burnt Lands Brook, already mentioned, has Mr. Thomas Boies, an active and enter-prising American, lately established a village, popu-larly called Boiestown after its founder. This village consists of 23 or 24 distinct buildings, embracing two excellent sawmills, a grist mill of the same character, a large forge with trip hammers, a washing mill, a cold and tepid bath, day school and private chapel, a re-spectable hotel, two ware rooms and a requisite num-ber of out offices. All the houses are well finished and neatly painted in the different varieties of white, red, green, yellow, etc., and this diversity of colours, coupled with the essential difference of shapes and figures, imparts an external sprightliness to the whole group, finely harmonizing with the animating sym-phony, proceeding from the various pursuits carried on within them.

This account of Boiestown, written in 1832, indicates that this small but central establishment had indeed flourished as a lumber town long before the building of the Canadian Eastern Railway line through here in 1883. At that time only the old stagecoach and portage route linked Boiestown to Fredericton and Chatham. In addition to the aforementioned buildings, Boiestown later could boast a blacksmith shop, a barber shop, two restaurants, a sled factory, a doctor's office, an undertaker, two dance halls and a weekly newspaper called the *Boiestown Record*, which was sold for five cents per issue. In

1901, the *Boiestown Record* stated, "Boiestown was the proud possessor of six general stores and two supply stores."

The village of Boiestown in 1890, as seen from the hilltop behind Mill Pond on Burnt Land Brook; a freight train is crossing the trestle. (*Public Archives of New Brunswick*)

But, like so many northeastern towns, Boiestown was built on a single industry—lumbering. Woodsworking was the chief source of livelihood for almost everyone in the town, from the shopkeepers and hotel owners to the millworkers and the lumberjacks themselves. An asset, of course, was Boiestown's location in the heart of prime virgin forest; and the wild rivers merging with the Miramichi, such as the nearby Taxis River and Burnt Land Brook, were all good driving streams. Transportation of lumber to the Boiestown sawmills from logging operations in the distant woods was by river driving, while sawed lumber would have been transported from the mills by river raft down the Miramichi. After the railway was built, much lumber was shipped by rail to Chatham for export, and Boiestown flourished.

The railway entered Boiestown over a high wooden trestle

which crossed Burnt Land Brook and advanced through the village's main street near the hotels and stores. One of these hotels was owned by Charles Duffy, and the accounts of Duffy's Hotel, with its splendid food and lodging and the atmosphere of chivalry, are nowadays still rendered in song and verse preserving Boiestown's exciting history.

Main Street Boiestown in early days. Duffy's Hotel is on the right, with guests sitting on the veranda. *(Public Archives of New Brunswick)*

Many old-timers in this region claimed credit for writing "Duffy's Hotel," but no one really knows the true author. The following is a version of the song as sung by Mrs. Crystal Young of Boiestown in 1960.

DUFFY'S HOTEL

If you're looking for fun and enjoyment
Or inclined to go out on a spree,

Come along with me over to Boiestown
On the banks of the Miramichi.
You'll meet with a royal reception;
My ventures to you I'll relate;
On the eighteenth of May I arrived here
From Fredericton—came on the freight.

I'm employed with a man, Edmund Kenney,
A gentleman who you know well,
J.P. for the parish of Stanley,
And he put up at Duffy's Hotel.

One night I went out on a party;
I tell you 'twas something immense;
We collared a shanghai rooster,
And he just cost us seventeen cents.
He was sick with the croup and the measles,
They said he was too poor for to sell,
But I guess he made hash for the boarders
That put up at Duffy's Hotel.

One night I went out on a party
Along with the rest of the boys.
We got full of Peely Island;
I tell you we made lots of noise.
We frightened the pigs up in Tugtown,
Caused the Pleasant Ridge dogs for to yell,
And when we got kicked out of Hayesville,
We struck 'er for Duffy's Hotel.
One night I went out on a party;
'Twas held in the mansion below;
A row was kicked up in the kitchen,
I tell you it wasn't too slow.
We upset the chairs and the tables;
The windows and stove, too, they fell.
This row was kicked up by Delaney,
A boarder at Duffy's Hotel.

Well friends, I must bid you good evening
For fear you will think me a turk.
If I linger 'round here any longer

Some fellow might give me a jerk!
I'll go back to the scenes of my childhood,
In peace and contentment to dwell;
Bid *adieu* to the kind entertainment
I met with at Duffy's Hotel.

Vignettes of Boiestown in the 1800s reveal this village as a bustling train stop, its hotels crowded with lumbermen *en route* to river drives or logging camps in the interior. On the street, the sounds of scraping fiddles were heard beneath the whooping from a rowdy Saturday-night dance hall.

One who came to work the lumber woods here in 1880 was Peter Emberley, a handsome youth from Prince Edward Island who had quarrelled with his father and, to his mother's grief, had left home. Everyone in the village of Boiestown liked young Peter. He was employed in a lumber camp with Dave McLellan but was fatally injured when a log from a yard fell upon him.

One of the men who was working with Emberley on that job was John Calhoun of Parkers Ridge, who would later become known for his folksongs. After the accident, Calhoun and Dave McLellan's son Alex brought Peter out to the settlement. On the way out of the woods the injured boy, who was lying on a camp sled pulled by a team of horses, rambled on in delirium about his home in P.E.I., his mother and his stern father. He died at the McLellan home after several days of suffering.

Peter Emberley was a Catholic, but deep snow prevented a priest from reaching Boiestown in time to officiate at his funeral. However the whole village attended and a layman read the burial service.

Peter Emberley's grave is located in the small cemetery just across the highway from the Central New Brunswick Woodsmen's Museum. John Calhoun's ballad of the tragedy is rated as possibly the best of the Miramichi folksongs.

PETER EMBERLEY

My name is Peter Emberley
As you may understand,
I was born on Prince Edward Island

Near to the ocean strand.
In eighteen hundred and eighty,
When the flowers were a brilliant hue,
I sailed away from my native isle
My fortune to pursue.

I landed in New Brunswick
In a lumbering country,
I hired to work in the lumber woods
On the sou'west Miramichi.
I hired to work in the lumber woods
Where they cut the tall spruce down,
While loading teams with yarded logs I
 Received a deadly wound.

There's danger on the ocean,
Where the waves roll mountains high.
There's danger on the battlefield
Where the angry bullets fly.
There's danger in the lumber woods
For death lurks sullen there,
And I have fell a victim
Into that monstrous snare.
I know my luck seems very hard
Since fate has proved severe,
But victor Death is the worst can come
And I have no more to fear.
And he'll allay those deadly pains
And liberate me soon,
And I'll sleep the long and lonely sleep
Called the slumber in the tomb.

Here's *adieu* to Prince Edward's Island
That garden in the seas,
No more I'll walk its flowery banks
To enjoy a summer's breeze.
No more I'll view those gallant ships
As they go swimming by
With their streamers floating on the breeze
Above the canvas high.

Here's *adieu* unto my father
It was him who drove me here,
I thought he used me cruelly
His treatments were unfair,
For 'tis not right to oppress a boy
Or try to keep him down,
'Twill oft repulse him from his home
When he is far too young.

Here's *adieu*unto my greatest friend,
I mean my mother dear,
She raised a son who fell as soon
As he left her tender care.
'Twas little did my mother know
When she sang lullaby,
What country I might travel in
Or what death I might die.
Here's *adieu* unto my youngest friends,
Those island girls so true,
Long may they bloom to grace that isle
Where first my breath I drew.
For the world will roll on just the same
When I have passed away,
What signifies a mortal man
Whose origin is clay?

But there's a world beyond the tomb
To it I'm nearing on,
Where man is more than mortal
And death can never come.
The mist of death it glares my eyes
And I'm no longer here
My spirit takes its final flight
Unto another sphere.

Tragedies such as this were common in the tough life of the
woodsman and quite often a song would be put together to
mark the event. At social gatherings or even in the lumber

camps, those present found a form of solace as well as entertainment in reliving the incident. It was a sharing of grief and superstition. Most woods foremen, however, would not allow the singing of "Peter Emberley" in their camps. It was said to bring bad luck.

Other entertainment in the old days came with the circus to Boiestown. It was said that Boiestown hosted many circuses because of its central location in the province and its accessibility by rail.

Someone wrote: "Having spent the night in Boiestown and having had food and drink at Duffy's where I was lodging, I awoke in the morning to the frightening sounds of lions and tigers howling in the street below my window. I thought I was having a mad dream, caused from my own affliction of hooch, the night before. But at the window, I observed that it was indeed an actual circus."

Today the attraction in Boiestown is New Brunswick's Central Woodsmen's Museum, an extensive collection of lumbering artifacts that brings to life these segments of Boiestown's active past. This is a village proud of its age-old traditions, its heritage of gallant lumberjacks and log-driving rivermen working the wild rivers of the upper Miramichi. The museum is a statement of pride in that glory gone.

3
DOAKTOWN

Doaktown is sited on the river's south side at Pine Island, some twenty miles downstream from the village of Boiestown. The river road (Hwy. #8) winds through the village and for a distance becomes Doaktown's main street.

Early photograph of Main Street, Doaktown. *(Belva Brown)*

The business district is made up of such facilities as service stations, stores, churches, schools, bank and doctor's office, as well as a curling club, bowling lanes, legion hall and a public library. There are two police stations: RCMP and the NB Highway Patrol detachments.

For tourists, there is a spanking new nine-hole golf course, museums such as the Doak House and the Miramichi Salmon Museum, motels and a good country inn. Doaktown is located in the heart of some of the best Atlantic salmon water you'll find in North America and there are river outfitters within the town limits to serve travellers. Guides and equipment can be acquired through the outfitters.

The town's chief employer is the lumber mill, owned by Russell and Swim, which is located just outside the town. This mill was established in 1922 and now employs 75 full-time millworkers with an additional 75 part-time employees working in the woods operations. This mill produces mainly sawed lumber and has always kept forest conservation a top priority. Even today, in certain new growth, forest machinery is not allowed and horses are used to yard logs. The economy of Doaktown depends a good deal on the mill. Through Swim and Russell's efficiency, Doaktown has shown steady growth and could be the Miramichi's most prosperous little town.

It is said that the first settlers to arrive in Doaktown in the later part of the 17th century were a handful of Frenchmen who fled upriver to escape the British. The *Doaktown Review* dated March 28, 1902, states that "the French didn't stay long in Doaktown, leaving the area to the Indians when peace between the countries was restored." There is little evidence of English-speaking settlers on the upper reaches of the Miramichi before the American Revolution. Ephraim Betts, a sergeant in Delaney's Regiment had gone to Fredericton in 1783 and kept a shop there until 1795, when he moved to Miramichi seeking new adventure. Being a Connecticut Loyalist, Betts had gained a tract of land in Miramichi between the portage route leading from the Nashwaak and a lot reserved above the Etienne (Cains) River. This is where Doaktown stands today.

By 1799, Betts had established a settlement which was formally registered on June 20th, 1809, as the first allocation of land on the upper southwest Miramichi River. Sixty families were inhabiting the upper settlement area of what was still known as the Parish of Newcastle. All of these families were under the leadership of Betts, who later became Overseer of Fisheries, Commissioner of Roads, Overseer of the Poor and eventually Justice of the Peace.

One of the families under Betts's leadership was Ben Davis and his sister, who arrived in 1807 and settled in the general vicinity of where the Doaktown High School stands today.

Here they constructed two log houses a short distance apart. They undertook to build the region's first hotel, whipsawing the boards by hand and hewing out the framework. Two years later, the building was completed and in use. This hotel remained in Doaktown for many years, eventually becoming the home of a Mr. Attridge.

By this time, the land was being cleared slowly and wheat was being raised and ground by hand into flour. They were also bringing in livestock. Someone wrote: "It is almost impossible for a farmer to keep sheep in pastures here, because of the great numbers of hungry bears."

The Miramichi region at this time was an immense forest of tall, straight pine trees. All large pines of a certain size and length were reserved for king's masts and a mark, the "broad arrow," was placed on them by scouts who cruised them out and took a "spawl" of the tree's trunk with a broad axe, driving the brand into it with a pole axe or sledge hammer. These trees were not to be used for anything but the Royal Navy. Some of the river's first English-speaking settlers, such as William Davidson of Elm Tree, were agents designated to harvest these trees. An immense industry began in the pine mast business. These were shipped overseas by the ton.

The old *Doaktown Review* stated that in 1815 Ben Davis built Doaktown's first blacksmith shop and the settlement's first gristmill was built three years later by a Mr. McAllister. This mill was water-driven. In 1822, the first schoolhouse was built, a crude structure that would later be used by the Russell family as a pigpen. It was said that the nearest trustee of that school was some twenty miles down the river at Blackville.

There were no churches built in the region at this time ... and preachers travelled from house to house giving sermons. One such preacher was a Rev. Mr. McCurdy, a Methodist patriarch whose main concern was the folly of the times. It was said that McCurdy was so straight-laced that he even objected to the young ladies blackening their shoes or wearing a bit of ribbon in their home-made straw hats.

Everyone on the Miramichi was travelling by horseback or canoe. It was said that when it came to judging horseflesh, some of the women were better at it than the men. Many of the women were as strong as men and could reap grain with a sickle and were experts with a whipsaw.

Their homes were log huts, with no stoves, just the large stone fireplaces which were also the only source of heat. Matches were scarce. If someone in the neighbourhood let his fire burn out by accident, he would have to run to the nearest neigbour for a live coal.

The 1902 *Doaktown Review* also stated that there was much poverty in the early settlements. If someone in a household was fortunate enough to own a pair of fine dress shoes, so highly were these regarded that if one were going to a social gathering in the area, the shoes would be carried in a bag and put on in the yard outside the house where the party was. People in a household often shared such common things as hairnets or a pair of spectacles.

By this time too, the women were beginning to spin and weave the different Miramichi plaids. Someone wrote that "the upriver plaids are the larger ones and the farther up the river, the larger the plaids."

In 1820, a scow ferry was established and was operated by Henry Swim, crossing the river where the highway bridge is located today. The fee for the ferry passage was twenty cents for a horse and carriage and five cents for each person. Swim was a young man who had come to the area at the age of seven years. It was said that a man had left him with Ben Davis while he took a trip to Chatham. The man never returned. Young Henry grew up to be a fine gentleman, eventually marrying the sister of Squire Doak, the man for whom Doaktown was named. The Swim ferry was operated until 1847 when the first bridge was built across the river.

At this time the mail was carried on horseback by the postmaster himself, and the government was surveying the Great Road which was to be cut out through the woods from Fredericton to Newcastle. In the spring of 1823, Squire Robert Doak was appointed Overseer of Highways for the district. He supervised the construction as turnpiking began, with wooden bridges spanning the ravines and the deep-gulched wild streams of the stagecoach trail that would bring commu-nication between the two larger centres. The Great Road was a difficult task as machinery was nil and men had to construct trestles and dykes literally by hand. Through the barrens and the swampland, logs were cut and laid side by side in a "corduroy road" choked with brush and sods to fill the cracks. This route, which connected the regions with mail and passenger service, remained in use for some sixty years, until the coming of the railway in the 1880s. It is said that sections of the old stage trail are still visible as a ridge of moss through the woods, unused for over a century.

In his article, "The Wild East," published in *The Atlantic Advocate* in 1987, Richard Doyle wrote: "Travelling by stagecoach in the Maritimes, found most roads difficult, if not perilous, at any time of the year. When the roads were at their worst it was often necessary to resort to some ingenious expedient in order to ascend a steep hill. Heavy ropes secured to a stout tree on a hilltop were occasionally used by the driver (and his passengers) to assist the horses in hauling the coach up a steep incline where the roadway was washed out by heavy rains. On other occasions, horses and men combined to raise the front wheel out of a deep hole. It was quite usual for the passengers to help pry the coach out of the mud and to walk a considerable part of the journey."

Of the stage stops along the Great Road, Doyle wrote: "The hostels along the stagecoach routes could often supply a comfortable haven for the weary passenger, but in general there was not much romantic about the ordinary run of taverns and inns which dotted the countryside. Too often they were the scene of drunkenness, and many early travellers spoke of beds so dirty or full of bugs that it was preferable to either lie on the floor or keep travelling during the night."

In 1824, the first official census showed 154 families in the district. There were 156 houses with an additional eighteen under construction. The parish contained 1,200 people with the most important man in the district being Squire Doak.

By 1834, the huge parish of Ludlow had been subdivided into the parishes of Ludlow, Blissfield and Blackville.

The 1840s brought a great recession to the area and many families moved from the Miramichi to the State of Maine. Some had lost their farms, having mortgaged them for cash or farming materials or both.

In 1855, the first official schoolteacher arrived in Doaktown: one Burke Archibald, who later gave up teaching to go into lumbering. For a time, Archibald had supplied a scow service between Doaktown and Newcastle.

In the 1880s came the railroad, with its huge river trestle right beside the covered highway bridge. This added growth to Doaktown with its freight and passenger service. The trains meant easy access to merchandise for storekeepers and for lumbermen and mill operators. It meant quick transportation to the larger centres, the city of Fredericton or the seaport at Chatham. Passengers travelled to Doaktown from the small train stops in the remote settlements. They came for entertainment, for church services, to see a doctor or to appeal to a Mountie to settle a squabble.

There were many boardinghouses in Doaktown around the turn of the century. Lumbermen came with their teams of horses to haul logs or spoolwood, some to the main river for driving, some to local mills and some to the railway cars. One boarding place was the Aberdeen Hotel operated by the Swim family, perhaps the largest building in Doaktown. The Aberdeen was a three-storey Klondike-style hotel, false-fronted with many verandas and balconies decorated with spool railings. As well as its rooms for rent, the building housed a general store, the post office and the private residence of William White. The Aberdeen burned to the ground in 1925, catching on fire in the middle of a windy October night and taking a half-dozen smaller buildings with it. Firemen struggled as the entire village was threatened. There were no casualties.

But the most famous boardinghouse in Doaktown was the Gilks House. This farmhouse-style dwelling was built in 1890 by Allen Doak and used as a private home. It changed hands several times. George Hinton, who owned it for a short time, sold it to Mr. and Mrs. James Gilks who ran it as a hotel. The Gilks House became famous for its good food and lodging. In 1939, when King George VI and Queen Elizabeth were touring Canada, they stopped here for food and relaxation. The house was later owned by Mrs. Percy Crocket, who in turn sold it to William McKinnon, who offered the house to be used as a museum or historic site. It was closed due to a lack of government funding and the building has since been sold again and converted to apartments.

THE OLD STAGE ROAD

There it stretches away
Through the dark and silent woods,
The road where the stage-coach used to run;
But for many dreary days
None have walked its weary ways
From the rising to the setting of the sun.

The deer and the moose
Now its darkened paths do tread,
While the branches of the trees shut out the sky;
But I love it just the same,—
It has been a path to fame
Of many who now in the grave do lie.

CHORUS:

Even now I hear the rattle
Of the wheels upon the hillside;
Even now I hear the cheery voice
Of him the driver old,—
Teaming proudly on the horses
As they champ their bits and whinner,
Whinner for they know 'tis supper time
And they are near the fold.

Oh well do I remember
The driver, poor old man,
He often with us over night did stay;
But one morn he was found dead—
'Twas old age, the people said—
Yes, the angels they had ta'en his soul away.

Ah! but those were happy days
When the old stage used to run,
When the rich man amongst us was unknown;
We were happy and content,
And a kind word was well meant

To comfort the cheerless and alone.

But they'll never come again to us,
Those dear and bygone days,
There [sic] glories now are vanished like a dream;
And the people, too, likewise,
Have been gathered to the skies,
As the ocean holds the clear and crystal stream.

- Jardine

4
THE DOAK HOUSE

The Doak House is situated at the northeast end of Main Street in the village of Doaktown. This quaint house was built in the early 1800s by a Scotsman named Robert Doak. It has become an historic site (with the house and barn completely restored to their original charm through government grants), staffed with guides and caretakers during the tourist season. The old house is a monument honouring Squire Doak, the hard-working pioneer businessman who became a chief magistrate and gave his name to the village: Doakton and later Doaktown.

Early photograph of the Doak House and property, with a saw mill across the highway. *(Author's Collection)*

It was here, in this dwelling, that the Squire performed wedding ceremonies and made land settlements for the villagers. He was indeed respected, a symbol of justice representing the region's government. He later made a gift to the village of the land where the Baptist Church and elementary school now stand.

Across the street from his home, he built and operated a carding mill, kiln and gristmill. The two huge circular stones that ground the grain in the gristmill came over from France by ship as ballast. Sir Samuel Tweedie and other distinguished gentlemen of the day would often come many miles for the coarse-ground flour that this mill produced. Later, a sawmill was built in the same general area. The mills operated by water power from a big water wheel that was driven from a brook-fed millpond. It was said that if the Squire's son James Andrew had lived, there would have been a spinning jenny added to the mill.

The mill was dismantled in 1925 by Hubert Edison Doak and sold to Henry Ford. It is believed that much of its antique machinery is now on exhibit among other collected pieces in Greenfield Village or in the main museum building at Dearborn, Michigan.

But the wood-framed house itself stands in its original form. Very little is changed in architecture or in mood. It is set back from the village street just enough to feature a small short-clipped front garden. Bedding flowers and shrubs of old lilac and plum frame the building, with its whitewashed siding, and clinging creeper vines grow around the French windows and the garden fences.

The Doak property also included several hundred acres of farmland which supplied grain as well as wool and lumber for the district. They raised 100 hogs annually and kept cattle and teams of horses.

The house has solid oak doors with huge square locks, which were installed partly for elegance and partly for safety. It was said that the Squire's wife was afraid of Indians and that the builders took particular care for her safety. The parlor was almost a fort, with window shutters over one inch thick that slide into the wall when not in use.

Much of the furniture in the Doak House was imported

from the old country. A huge grandfather clock, inherited by Mrs. Doak from her ancestors in Scotland, had to be shortened by a craftsman to accommodate the low ceilings so common in New Brunswick. In the parlor there is a settee of elegantly scrolled wood with tufted velvet upholstery. The beds in this house are rustic, patch-quilted and somewhat shorter than today's beds. There are also old trunks, pictures, china and kitchen utensils displayed.

Squire Doak died in 1857 from cancer of the face. The superstitious said it was the curse put upon him by a drunken sailor (deserting his ship on Miramichi Bay to get a ship on the Bay of Fundy) who was refused his hospitality.

In 1983, the Central Miramichi Historical Society acquired a government grant of $145,228, through a Canada Community Development Project, to restore and develop the Doak House and surrounding farm buildings. Eventually the old mills will also be restored. The province of New Brunswick (Department of Tourism, Recreation and Heritage) provided research personnel to train and direct the project workers, and contributed funds to help promote this project.

5
THE MIRAMICHI
SALMON MUSEUM

The Miramichi Salmon Museum is a building in the style of a fishing lodge that sits on a slope overlooking the river in the village of Doaktown. Built in 1983, this project was a top priority when Doaktown's Miramichi Historic Society was formed in 1973.

The Miramichi River long has been rated as the world's greatest salmon river and the Atlantic salmon has put the region on the map. The Society thought it fitting to construct a world-class salmon museum here in the geographic centre of the river's fly-fishing reaches.

To encourage the project, in 1982 the federal and provincial governments awarded grants of $228,000 and $115,000 respectively toward the museum's construction. It was opened the following spring.

The Miramichi Salmon Museum is a unique tourist attraction where salmon enthusiasts celebrate the existence of this noble gamefish.

This region has always depended to some degree on the tourist industry. Each summer, visitors arrive in great numbers to experience what is considered the best sports fishing: the catching of the Atlantic salmon with a rod and reel.

The museum was a community project. W.R. McKinnon, a Doaktown businessman, donated the 3 1/2-acre riverside property. In addition, $50,000 was raised through donations and local fund-raising campaigns.

The museum features sundecks and windows that overlook the natural habitat of the Atlantic salmon. There are sandstone fences, flower beds, and a fireplace adding to the camp atmosphere. There are also a smokehouse, an icehouse, a boathouse, woodsheds, outhouses and a guide's camp.

Inside, the museum features a display of live Atlantic salmon in an aquarium designed to display the fish's development in its various stages. There are a fly-tying bench, a poacher's corner, a guide and outfitter section, a fishing photo and film exhibit, and various artifacts. There is a banquet facility accommodating 140 people, and each year new members are inducted into the Miramichi Salmon Hall of Fame.

The museum's objectives are to interpret the impact of the Atlantic salmon on the Miramichi region, past, present and future, to educate people in the importance of the Atlantic salmon as a species and as a gamefish and resource, and to promote conservation and good sportsmanship.

Other activities provide river excursions ranging from a few hours to a few days, a fly-fishing school, and the teaching of canoeing and guiding techniques.

Outside the museum, in season, the salmon can be seen as they leap and play while returning home to spawn. The turbulent, brawling, fast-water pools of the Miramichi with their abundance of this exciting gamefish have kept a tourist flow here since the turn of the century. The squires and land dealers who once lived here gave grants of land along the river for the promise of working the land and establishing family farms. For these settlers, the river was the only means of communication, and to encourage new settlers, promises were made of fresh caribou, moose, and plenty of salmon.

It has been said that a man standing on a rock at the top of Wildcat Pool, on the Northwest Miramichi, could spear a winter's supply of salmon for the entire community in a single evening.

The Atlantic salmon is recognized as a valuable resource throughout the entire eastern seaboard. It plays an important role in the economy of the towns and villages of the Miramichi.

For the river-folk and those who follow the migration of the Atlantic salmon, the Miramichi Salmon Museum is a kind of shrine, a place to visit to discover more about this challenging gamefish and to celebrate it.

6
THE CARR VIOLIN

When Doaktown's William Carr was twelve years old he made a fiddle: a wooden cigar box bridged with gut strings, a hand-carved finger board and four wooden pegs. That was in 1915. Since then he has built dozens of violins, some of which are being played by amateur and professional fiddlers throughout the east, and William Carr has earned a reputation as a skilled violin maker.

As a boy growing up in Doaktown, Carr studied violin under Thomas Ross, the renowned violin teacher from Blackville. He learned to read music and reach the difficult scales.

In 1928, as a young woodsman working the log drives on the Bartholomew, Carr constructed another fiddle. This was a crude makeshift violin built from a tin cooking pan, using the pan's handle as a finger board, with wooden pegs fixed on the end to tighten the gut strings. The violin bow used on that instrument was a tree branch bowed in a hoop with horse hair stretched tightly, and it was sawed into melted-down pitch from a black spruce for rosining. With this, Willie Carr entertained the men with jigs and reels around the cooking tents during the evenings. In later years he would play semi-classical music, performing with a church orchestra as well as at many dance halls and social functions throughout the Miramichi region. Carr had become a reputable violinist himself and, as it turned out, this would be a kind of apprenticeship for his unique hobby as a violin maker.

William Carr has always been a fine carpenter by trade, save for the odd job over the years in the lumber woods or at the sawmill. In 1934, at Holmes's sawmill in Doaktown, he lost three fingers from his left hand, ending his violin practice. It was at this time that Carr turned to violin building as a serious pastime.

He built himself a small workshop behind his house, acquired a collection of working tools, chisels and clamps from a blacksmith friend and proceeded in good earnest to seek out the proper material for the best-sounding violins. This, he found, was well-seasoned, dry, sound lumber straight in grain, the pieces matched in their variations of thicknesses. This helps to produce an almost invisible seam when the work is finished to his satisfaction.

At the slow pace of one violin each winter, Mr. Carr hand-carves each individual piece of selected quality wood, carefully steaming and moulding their curvatures, carving out the heads and applying clamps and special glues to join them. Then he sands and varnishes.

Many of the materials used by Carr are similar to those used by professional violin makers around the world. The three-piece violin back is carved from white maple. The top is spruce, the finger board and tuning pegs are ebony, and only the best of violin varnishes are acquired from Carr's suppliers in Montreal. Top-grade strings are also used. Attachments such as tail pieces, E-string adjusters, bridges and chin rests are purchased from music supply stores in Fredericton. At one point, Carr used to hand-carve even the smallest of detailed attachments, but nowadays he finds it much simpler and less expensive to purchase these from a factory.

It was said that Willie Carr once built a fiddle from dried lumber he salvaged from a demolished Baptist Church manse. "That made a good instrument for playing hymns on," joked Carr. Some of the material used now is imported from Germany.

Today, the Carr violin is a sophisticated instrument. All constructed in the 4/4 full size (he does not like the smaller 3/4 or 1/2 size instruments) they have a rich mellow sound, are handsome in appearance and are accurate to scale. Indeed, the Carr violin is as fine a violin by many standards as any made in the country—a product resulting from many hours of meticulous craftsmanship.

Aged 83, William Carr is still enthralled by the art of violin making. He spends his creative energy in short intervals in the workshop. Since the mill accident, he has had to learn how to play his fiddle all over again, using the forefinger and stubs on his left hand. While testing his instruments for scale, he can still treat a visitor to some toe-tapping jigs and reels.

7
THE BUTTERFLY HOOK

The late Jack Sullivan was an outfitter and river guide who lived in the small community of Blissfield on the Miramichi River.

In his farmhouse and adjacent cabins he hosted guests during the angling seasons, generally non-residents, fly-fishermen who came to the Miramichi in search of the Atlantic salmon.

Guiding their rushing canoes through the churning rapids and across the gleaming lakes of the Miramichi was a way of life for Sullivan. He loved the field work and, like a Scout leader at camp, he preached conservation and the ethics of the outdoor sports.

He taught many a novice adventurer the ways of the river, how to handle a canoe, flycast and camp in the wilderness. Spirited campfire songs, the singing of spinning reels and the splash of a battling salmon became familiar sounds to the outfitter.

But the short-lived angling season of the northeast soon passes. The bumping ice floes that crowd the rivers immediately following the October fishery send the river people hustling south.

The country becomes barren as the river freezes above the spawning salmon. The beautiful summits along the riverbank, visited by passing canoemen throughout the angling season, are now silent. The hush is broken only by the hammering woodpecker or the scream of a whisky-jack.

To an outfitter and guide like Sullivan, it meant several months without work. Until mid April, he had the long winter to pass waiting for ice-out.

Over the years Sullivan worked at various jobs at lumber

camps, sawmills and construction sites. But some twenty years ago he found a hobby in fly-tying. During the winter months he produced quantities of salmon flies for fishermen up and down the eastern seaboard.

Some of the fly patterns tied at Sullivan's cabin were called bugs, bombers, rat faces, wulffs, nymphs and streamers. But the most common flyhook in the shop was the Ingalls butterfly.

The butterfly was invented in the early 1960s by American Maurice Ingalls. He was an old crony of Sullivan's and stayed for a time at the latter's cabin.

Having learned firsthand the hook pattern and its potential, Sullivan began tying butterflies for anglers in the United States and Canada. Local anglers could acquire them at general stores and service stations throughout the Miramichi valley which displayed both the butterfly and variations of the original design.

Once an outfitter on the Miramichi River himself, Ingalls kept a guest camp in what is now known as the Ted Williams swinging-bridge pool area. That's where he put together the first stages of the butterfly. It's a slow-water hook and was designed for the Big Southwest Miramichi River at the Ingalls camp.

The original stages of the pattern consisted of a black yarn body on a number 5 hook and two 45-degree-angle wings of white goat hair. The flexible wings would gyrate through the water when retrieved properly. The motions resemble movements of a water bug or a swimming insect. Sullivan claimed that Ingalls had fished the basic butterfly idea successfully for years before releasing word of his invention. During that time, Ingalls experimented. Eventually he presented the idea to Wallace Doak, the late tackle-shop owner and fly-tier from Doaktown.

Doak agreed that the pattern showed promise, but he changed the body from the black yarn to a peacock herl and added brown hackle feathers. The Ingalls butterfly was born.

Seasoned salmon anglers on the Miramichi River were reluctant to try the strange-looking hook. Having used the conservative feathered classics successfully, they frowned on the ugly butterfly. But the pattern was not to be denied its place in the angling world, and soon it appeared in showcases and tackle boxes, pushing aside many old patterns.

On the rivers, the Ingalls butterfly was catching salmon in almost all conditions and as word of its capabilities swept the salmon world, the demand grew.

Distributors, fly-tiers, shopkeepers, outfitters and river guides as well as the anglers sought out the pattern. The butterfly encouraged a feeling of confidence because its catch average went beyond that of any other salmon fly in history.

For the tackle shop owner, it was a commodity offering high turnover and quick profits. For the fly-tier like Sullivan, it kicked off an era known as "the butterfly boom."

After the Ingalls years, Sullivan tied many thousands of butterflies, some of which are variations of the original pattern. They are now tied to various-sized hooks with multi-coloured bodies. They have slim or large bodies for slow and fast water respectively. In fast water the large body gives the hook the appearance of a nymph as the heavy current closes the wings.

As a result of the boom, goat hair has become scarce and many shops have had to substitute white hair from other domestic farm animals to create the distinctive wings of the fly.

While anglers in eastern Canada and the United States review their inventory of flyhooks for the spring season, in Sullivan's small cabin the woodstove kept a steady heat as the smoke-pipe creaked and rattled in the wind.

Sullivan crouched over an ancient rolltop desk, its drawers jammed with coloured yarn, hooks, thread and a thousand feathers. Lighting a cigarette, he poured a coffee and began to wrap yarn on a bare hook. His plaid shirt, suspenders and drooped mustache marked him as a riverman.

To his right on the desk was a cigar box containing hundreds of butterflies. Like so many insects, they had a short life expectancy. Some retired to fly cases, never to be used again after taking trophy-sized Atlantic salmon. Others were traded among anglers who swap flies at the river's edge as they exchange fishing tales.

For Sullivan the rewards were small, but it was a good hobby that kept him at the summer camp year-round. That's reward enough.

8
BLACKVILLE

Blackville is a bright village seated on the north riverbank, about twenty miles upstream from Newcastle at the mouth of the Bartholomew River. The population here varies around 1,000.

Officially incorporated as a village in 1967, it's a typical modern-day community with fast-food outlets, self-serve filling stations, a volunteer fire and ambulance service, and a police patrol. It also has a sprawling modern high school, a legion hall, a half-dozen churches, modern fairgrounds and recreational facilities and a new water and sewage system.

On the southwest end of Main Street (Highway #8) stands the sawmill, its yard dappled with yellow skids of sweet-scented sawed lumber. The mill is the main employer here, with 80 workmen at the plant and some 200 woodsworkers on logging operations in the forest. On working days the snarls and rattles of the sawmill echo through the village streets. The noises from the mill, with its shrill lunch whistle, have been comforting sounds to the people of Blackville since the early 1800s. This village has steadily progressed in the protective shadow of the mill. Thus, a circular saw and a green tree, featured above a lumber pile, are displayed on the town's welcome sign, a symbol of its livelihood.

This is New Brunswick's official logging town, having chosen that identity on its incorporation. Each July, the New Brunswick Loggers Show is held here; there is a parade through the streets and the crowning of a logging queen. This is followed by a canoe race, power-saw cutting contest and various forms of entertainment and contests related to the lumber woods.

Early photograph of three Blackville mills. The old water-powered lumber mill is to the right. The first steam-powered mill is in the rear, with the water-powered grist mill to the left. Note the village in the background, with its churches, and the street lined with picket fences. *(Blackville Historical Society)*

Since the coming of the first settlers, the principal centre of the lumber industry has been in Northumberland County and Blackville has a long history of sawmills.

The first known mills here were built in 1820 by two Scotsmen, a Mr. Doak and Alexander McLaggan. This was ten years before the parish of Blackville was established by Hon. William Black, an administrator for the government of New Brunswick and the fourth mayor of Saint John. The Doak/McLaggan mill was located on the riverbank and operated by a water wheel which drove a set of gang saws, and lath and shingle machines. This was always referred to as the "old water mill." Later, on the opposite side of the river, a gristmill was established; but it had to close in 1902 for economic reasons and because of its outdated, inefficient machinery.

Around 1893, Alexander (Boss) Gibson, a Nashwaak industrialist, took over the water mill and built a steam mill in the same general area. The high brick chimney built at this time was then, at 82 feet, the highest in New Brunswick. When this chimney was officially completed in the autumn of 1893, a young workman by the name of Tom Curtis climbed to the top and stood on his hands on the chimney rim, to the delight of the celebrating village. This chimney remained standing until 1978 when government officials felt it had become a safety hazard.

In 1883, Alex Gibson and Chatham's J.B. Snowball joined together in their entrepreneurship and built the Fredericton/Newcastle Railway Line (Canadian Eastern Railways) which ran near the mill yard.

Gibson was a stocky man with a long flowing beard. He got to know most of his employees personally and was well-respected by all the villagers. It was said that Boss Gibson always visited the schoolhouse on his visits to the Blackville mill. He would walk through the schoolyard with a pocket full of shiny new dimes passing them out to 60 or 70 students and commenting on how much they looked like their mothers or fathers.

Around 1915, Gibson sold the mill to the Nashwaak Pulp and Paper Company Limited. They took the railway as well. A Scotsman by the name of Archibald Alcorn was the manager as well as the financier for this company.

Archie Alcorn, for a time, was a kind of aristocrat in the village of Blackville. His elaborate and spacious home (today a country inn) was located in the most scenic part of the village, overlooking the broad millpond above the old milldam on the Bartholomew River. There was a high standard of social life at the Alcorn manor. Here lumbering businessmen and stylish acquaintances of Alcorn's mingled at frequent social functions. There were always a number of race horses in the adjacent livery stables.

The Alcorn mill was destroyed by fire in 1931. All that remained was a fireproof boiler and the chimney.

During the Gibson and Alcorn years, the village showed considerable progress and for a time it even boomed through its lumbering and sawmill operations. At one point Blackville could boast such businesses as a furniture store, jewellery shop, tailor, boot shop, taxidermy and barbering parlors, blacksmith, general stores, cheese factory, the Royal Bank and the Bank of Nova Scotia. There were also a doctor's office, drugstore, three hotels and an undertaker, as well as an indoor rink and a dance hall. Blackville had its own weekly newspaper (*The Advertiser*) which was edited by R.M. Grindlay and sold for two cents a copy.

Alcorn House in Blackville is now used as a country inn. (*Author's Collection*)

After the Alcorn era, the old mill property was leased to the Bamford brothers of Doaktown who built another mill and operated it successfully for several years. It was taken over in 1958, along with the woodlands, by a local firm called Miramichi Forest Products.

In 1973, fire destroyed this mill and the modern plant that exists today was constructed at its present location at the end of the village. The new mill was built by Hugh John Flemming and came under the Flemming/Gibson name. It operated until 1977 when it was closed and in turn sold to the Rayonier people, an American firm. In 1987, this mill was purchased by another local group and its name changed to Nautical Terra

Inc. With the exception of a couple of shutdowns because of poor market conditions, this mill has operated with success.

While this Miramichi village has had its share of lean years, the livelihood of these people has generally grown brighter, leaning on the stability of the sawmill. Mayor Roland Walls is expecting future growth through spin-offs from the maximum-security federal prison recently constructed at nearby Renous. The village council also has plans for a new medical clinic with a full-time doctor and nurses to assist in regional health care. The Blackville Historical Society is in the planning stages for construction of an old-fashioned water mill. This would be located on the riverbank, where the village's first mill was built in 1920, and would operate as a kind of museum, featuring artifacts pertaining to the village's mill history.

For the present, however, as has been the case throughout history, the village's most valuable resource is the working sawmill and on workdays it can be heard throughout the village as it snarls and rattles and continues to bear the load.

9

THE RECITATIONS OF MARGUERITE CURTIS

For Marguerite A. Curtis, a "dialect reader" early in this century, it was a long road from a farm settlement on the Miramichi River to the lights of New York City's Carnegie Hall. The stage was her first love and few performers have gone so far from such humble beginnings.

Marguerite was born on February 14th, 1866, in Gray Rapids, and grew up the oldest daughter in a family of ten children. As a young girl, she attended the local country schoolhouse and many times would have to miss classes to help around the farm. Like her young playfellows, she found entertainment romping through the fields or taking excursions for wild flowers. But Marguerite also loved to read and she would recite to the family. These readings became regular social gatherings in the Curtis household. Later, she would have her brother William build her a reading platform of scraps of boards nailed between the trees in their backyard. Here on summer evenings Marguerite would read for groups of family and neighbours. Years later Marguerite wrote, "The acceptance of those readings was as meaningful to me then as the ovations from the greater stages as an adult."

As a teenager, Marguerite developed into an attractive brown-eyed, curly-haired blonde. Singing as well as reciting, she was performing at dance halls along the Miramichi. In Blackville, violin professor Thomas Ross described her as "a rare talent." Known for her versatility, she could impersonate many singers of that day. She could also mimic a variety of song birds. But her rise to fame would be as a dialect reader and by 1910 she had captivated audiences in many of America's best concert halls.

1890s photograph of dialect reader Marguerite Curtis as she worked at flower design in Boston. (*Review Book*)

One stepping stone was a concert at the Old Arctic Rink in Fredericton. Her evening recital was ended with a love song entitled "Lonely and Blue I Am Leaving," which she rendered wih true emotion. The larger and more sophisticated city audience loved her as did the Miramichi people.

In 1890 Marguerite married Fredericton's Chip Chase and sometime later, hoop-skirted in 'nineties fashion, journeyed south with the man of her fancy, travelling to Saint John by train from where they sailed into a bustling Boston harbour.

The two acquired a place in Chelsey, a district near Boston. Marguerite took a job as a flower maker with the Dennison's Paper Company, designing and arranging paper flowers. Here her artistic qualities were an asset and her job as head designer remained secure while she studied at a private reading school owned by a Madame Berucho. Madame Berucho gave personal attention to Marguerite, helping her to master the art of dialect copying and directing her in gestures and finishing postures. Marguerite always credited Madame Berucho for much of her success.

She was now getting invitations to read at social functions and her workload of studies and performances, plus her job in flower design, left her little time for a home life: her marriage to Chase ended in divorce.

By the turn of the century, Marguerite Curtis was popular both in the Boston area and in New York as a dialect reader. She read in many of these cities' top concert halls and opera houses, including the famous Fanuel Hall of Boston. One of her reviews reads:

> Miss Curtis is a new aspirant for honours of the reading platform, she is certainly destined to meet with great success. She recited a short but very interesting sketch entitled, 'conjugal love' by Sharp and in response to a hearty encore gave humourous [sic] Irish sketches which delighted everyone. This number, with a Scotch, Dutch and child character piece which she recited later, seemed to place her on the very front rank of dialect readers in this country. The naturalness with which her selections were rendered was the crowning charm and it is not too much to say that she completely

captivated the audience and at once. Her voice is rich, her face full of expression, her gestures correct and her enunciation invariably distinct, and the beautiful floral gifts with which she was presented were well merited. She was assisted by Miss Marion Osgood, violinist, Mr. U.S. Kerr, one of Boston's most popular Bassos and Mr. Alfredo Di Pasa, pianist.

In 1908, Marguerite met Philip J. Blank, a prominent Boston businessman who owned a leather factory and a real estate business. Blank was greatly impressed with Marguerite and had been attending her readings. When she was scheduled to read at Boston's Fanuel Hall, he hired an artist to sit in the audience and paint Marguerite's portrait while she was on stage. Sometime later, at an evening reception, Blank presented Curtis with the portrait. Marguerite, at the age of 42, married Philip Blank. He was ten years her senior.

Philip and Marguerite moved to Winchester, Massachusetts (a Boston suburb) and into a spacious old home owned by Blank at 280 Highland Avenue. Here there was a huge property with stables and giant oak trees. They employed inside servants, a gardener and stable hands. Now in her forties, Marguerite continued to present readings under her professional name, Curtis.

It is said that when Miss Curtis was scheduled to read at New York's Carnegie Hall, she had been suffering from an inflamed appendix. On the night of her recital, she had to travel from Boston to New York by train and present her reading while suffering considerable pain. After her appearance, she was taken to a hospital for treatment. Marguerite, though not necessarily a strong person, had never failed to keep an appearance date.

On one occasion, she appeared on a Boston stage as Juliet in Shakespeare's *Romeo and Juliet*. She also had written some of her own songs and poetry, but it is not known if she ever used her own material on stage.

By middle age, Marguerite was encountering chronic health problems. She was turning down appearance invitations regularly, choosing a life of greater repose. Eventually she retired from public appearances entirely.

Her husband Philip died in 1924 and was buried in Massachusetts. From then, Marguerite lived alone with a number of
house pets, seldom appearing in public for any reason. Occasionally she was visited by a relative from Canada, such as her
brother William. In those years she also received visits from
George Frederick Clark, a cousin and a fellow New Brunswicker who had become a popular novelist.

At the age of 89, Marguerite was found, by a caretaker,
unconscious on the floor of her home. She died shortly
thereafter on the fourth day of July, 1953.

Her remains were sent by train to her old home community
on the Miramichi River where a wake was held (American
security guards nearby) at a funeral parlor in Blackville. After
a brief service on a breezy afternoon she was laid to rest. The
country churchyard in which she was buried was just a stone's
throw from where her brother William had built her the
reading platform some eighty years before.

Turn-of-the-century photograph of Tom Curtis *(right)* as he poses with his younger brother Silas. Taken in Newcastle in the spring, soon after Tom had his beard shaved off. Because of this, he always said, "it's a poor likeness." Author's Collection

10
TOM CURTIS

Before the turn of the century, the Miramichi River region was "wild and woolly" by reputation. Great physical strength in a man was considered a virtue and many of the region's younger men practiced the art of self-defence for their own amusement and prestige. Old-timers now give their accounts of memorable events and the men involved. Many of these have been tinted golden in memory by the distance in time and the magic in looking back. Bits and pieces of old chestnuts are sparked when the greater names are tossed about in homes of senior citizens. One such legendary strongman was Tom Curtis.

Tom was born in the Gray Rapids district, on the Miramichi River, in December of 1870. He was the son of David and Elizabeth (Harris) Curtis and one of a family of six boys and four girls.

Tom's strength was said to be equal to that of two men his size. It was said that in his youth he was a symbolic figure of strength and fitness.

He was a stocky, solid man of five feet eleven inches in height. He had thick shoulders and chest, a lean square face, piercing eagle eyes and thinning brown hair. His arms and hands were huge and he was known to have great quickness of both hand and foot.

He could walk on his hands across a floating boom of logs or turn a handspring on a log adrift in midstream. He could kick a nine-foot ceiling with both feet or turn a flying handspring with both hands in his pants pockets. So supple was he that he could drop a pocket handkerchief on the floor behind him and, bending over backwards, pick it up with his teeth. Until he was an old man he never opened gates on his farm but jumped over them. One witness said that he watched Tom Curtis, aged 70, hold one foot up behind him and use his supporting foot to kick a snowshoe from its resting place three pork barrels high.

In Fredericton's Wavely-Lorne Hotel, in 1892, Curtis kicked a nine-foot ceiling to win a bet that was put up by Alexander Gibson, the Marysville industrialist. The astonished hotel proprietor had the footprints in the ceiling framed as a novelty and they remained on display for sixty years.

In Campbellton, when Tom was working on the Restigouche boom, he entertained Sunday crowds by doing stunts on logs floating in the currents. He put on another act on the wharf using a half-dozen pork barrels, jumping into one from another, or rolling them about by cuffing them with his hands, his feet in the air. He had become known around the province for his acrobatics, but here on the Miramichi his reputation had grown mainly because of his strength.

In Blackville, when Tom was working on a mill chimney for Alex Gibson, witnesses watched him lift a 500-pound cask of lime into an express wagon. When the 82-foot mill chimney was officially completed, he walked on his hands around the top rim of the stack while the villagers celebrated.

And of course he had developed into a powerful puncher. In Chatham, in 1910, some friends registered him in a punching contest at the shop of Mr. Snowball. When Tom asked the clerk in charge how much the punching machine would stand, the reply was: "Don't you worry about breaking it, sir, she'll stand twenty hundred." Tom hit the machine a single crashing blow, breaking it into a thousand pieces and sending the clerk shouting in a fit of amazement, astonished by the strength he had witnessed.

Men seeking a fighting reputation occasionally challenged Tom. Tom was not a fighting man by nature and he loathed the fighting name. "It's nothing but a dog's name," he told a man who challenged him to fisticuffs.

While Tom avoided conflict whenever possible, if there was a question of fair play he would take charge and end a fight in a matter of seconds.

As a result, a reputation as a peacemaker built around him. He was often hired to keep order at elections, weddings, church socials, dances or wherever crowds gathered. When Tom was put in charge, it was said that an unruly gang of ten men would hush to a silence.

But those who knew Tom remember him as a kind-hearted, sensitive man. He wrote songs, liked poetry and music, and played the mouth organ and concertina. He could make a flute from a swamp reed (accurate to scale) and with this he would entertain the men on the river drives. Sometimes at social gatherings he would recite poetry. In the early years he had been influenced by his oldest sister, Marguerite, who had become a well-known reader in Boston at the turn of the century.

Some of Tom's early cronies were men like Jack and Birp Harris, Jack Colford and Joe Smith. It was said that Joe Smith and Tom were often invited to entertain at social events. Smith was able to make make music deep in his throat that resembled a church organ. Whenever the two got together at socials, Joe would "play" the organ and Tom would sing.

In 1896, Tom married Barbara Sullivan, a local girl ten years his junior.

After the wedding reception in Gray Rapids, Tom and Barbara left with their few prized possessions and journeyed by canoe up the Miramichi River several miles to the farm community of Howards. They moved into an abandoned farmhouse on a grant of land that Tom had inherited from his aunt, Sarah Nutbeam.

The house had been empty for years, the doors and windows broken out. Sheep from neighbouring farms were loafing about the house and porch. The newlyweds commenced the task of restoring the house and reclearing the land, preparing to raise a family. Their twelve children were delivered here and many of the births were without the assistance of a doctor. Both Tom and Barbara lived to a ripe old age.

While Tom may not rank among the Miramichi's great names, he still remains a symbol of the lumbermen and rivermen of the past. Even today, if you mention his name to the old boys along this river, they will say, "Now there was a man!"

11
JOHN BROPHY:
DEAN CANOEIST-GUIDE

Some years ago, on a morning in spring, an American sportsman left his Miramichi cabin and went out onto the river in search of Atlantic salmon. Throwing all caution to the wind, and without the assistance of a guide, he attempted to manoeuver a light canoe through the rushing waters of a river in peak flow to the salmon pool where he and a guide had fished during summer. He was never seen again. The old guides of the river agreed that the canoe had been pulled under by the strong currents. The craft had probably been anchored with the sportsman seated in the anchor end; such a judgement would be fatal if executed in fast water.

Most guides agree that the lack of canoeing fundamentals exercised by many boatmen is bordering on the criminal. The changes in a river from its gentle lazy moods of summer to the churning waters of a river in spring flow are too often underestimated. During the run-off, pools that once appeared as gentle riffs become foaming torrents.

To learn canoeing fundamentals, the professional canoeist is the best source of knowledge. One such man is John Brophy, a highly skilled canoeist and a river guide on the Miramichi for over fifty years.

Born on the Cains, a Miramichi tributary, John Brophy now lives in Blackville on the main stem. He's a tall, rangy riverman who sports a mackinaw and wide-brimmed hat, displaying all the earmarks of the typical guide. His bronze complexion and iron-grey hair, together with his slightly stooped frame, identify him as a man who has spent the greatest part of his lifetime as a woodsman and guide. Growing up on the Cains, he learned the river ways as a matter of necessity. He learned to canoe through turbulent waters where sometimes ice floes and extensive log-jamming were very much a reality. John would often canoe to the nearby community of Howards at the mouth of the Cains for schooling or Sunday mass. He grew up in a canoe.

John Brophy, a Miramichi guide for over 50 years. (*Author's Collection*)

While still in his teens, Brophy took his first job guiding at Charlie Wade's camp, a well-known fishing lodge near the mouth of the Cains. John's ability to handle fishermen and his gentlemanly conduct around the sports encouraged Wade to advance him to guide foreman, in charge of some twenty men. Among the pioneer river guides were men like George and John Vickers, Joe Brennan, George Hennessy, Sr. and John's uncle Joe Brophy. Younger guides of the day were John's brothers Patrick, Christopher and Joseph, as well as Stanley Furlong, Lawrence Burke, and Eldon Curtis.

John worked for Wade for over thirty years. He now holds the job of guide and caretaker for Cains River Enterprises, a salmon club on his old home stream. He also free-lances, guiding the occasional fishing enthusiast who arrives in the village seeking his services.

As a canoeman, John and his younger brother Patrick have won canoe races around the province. In 1959, representing the Wade Fishing Camp and Chestnut Canoes Limited, the Brophy boys won first place honours in a 62-mile race from Woodstock to Fredericton on the Saint John River. Entered were many canoeists from all over the province, one of whom was a provincial champion. Later that year they took second prizes in a Doaktown-to-Blackville race on the Miramichi.

His years on the river were not without adventure, and sometimes near-disaster. John recalls waiting for a party of sports to arrive by train one night in the late '40s. The train arrived at midnight, dropping off six New York City anglers on the plank platform at the Howards Station. Here they were greeted by their river companion. These well-liquored men in search of adventure were to be portaged by Brophy to distant cabins on the Miramichi and the Cains. The river had been rising day after day until it was almost bursting its banks. The upriver ice, the clean-off from the jams in the tributaries, was adrift. Oblivious to the danger, the sports put their confidence in the guide. John's professional reputation was at stake but it was for their lives that he was so much concerned. Canoeing those drunken men through the ice floes in the dark of night was possibly the most dangerous experience that John could recall.

Brophy has guided fishermen from thirty states, many of whom John recalls as "fine people." He tells of a nervous youngster from Boston who appeared unable to learn the skills of fighting a salmon on a fly rod. Whenever the large salmon that he had hooked appeared near the surface, he yelled for John to "scoop!" Trying to scoop an unplayed fish without the help of the angler isn't easy. One slight move could send the fish on a run to midstream and possible freedom. "It's like making love," says John. "You have to keep your cool."

A story was told at a sports banquet by a man from Washington who had fished the Cains with John Brophy as a guide. The two were camped on the riverbank. In the evening, while they were saying their prayers in the tent, a God-darn porcupine walked away with John's moccasins.

John once told a sport that he knew a fishing hole on the Cains where the fish were biting so well he had to get behind a tree on the riverbank to tie on the flyhook.

But the business of guiding is not an easy life and is considered dangerous by many. John has seen a man suffer a heart attack after battling a large salmon. He has seen a man die on the riverbank, leaving his guide helplessly trying to administer first aid. He has seen boats capsize in midstream, leaving fishermen and guides both clinging to half-submerged canoes in water temperatures just one or two degrees above freezing. He has seen canoes crushed in ice jams, caught by an ice floe in midstream. He has seen angry anglers who spent good money for a vacation on the country's best salmon river but couldn't catch a fish—they always blame the guide.

Still and all, when the sweet scents of the mayflower and the swamp willow waft in from the back swamps and ponds to blend with the familiar odour of woodsmoke drifting from a fishing camp, and through the spruce the winking river beckons in the sun, even the least observant folk can feel a pull to its gravel shores and sparkling spring pools.

After fifty years of river life, John Brophy is no exception. He launches his Chestnut canoe, with his guest of the day seated firmly in the bow, and paddles across the current. As he dips the paddle deep and uses it as a rudder, the canoe remains steady. Checking the shoreline for location, he eases the anchor slowly into the water. The rope slips through his hands and tugs over a varnished gunwale, jerking tight at the rope's end to a gentle sway of the bow. For his guest, a millionaire from the U.S., it's a long-awaited vacation; for Brophy, the guide, it's an extended holiday. Here on the river he continues to enjoy life. For John, that's top priority.

12
THE GUIDES OF
CHARLIE WADE

The fishing outfitter of the Miramichi River goes back to the turn of the century. The camps of that day, however, were limited to a scattered few fishing huts nestled along the rivers at choice locations and were enjoyed by a precious few rich Americans. Some of those old lodges were owned by folks like the Griffins or the Pratts. The sports fishery back then meant little to the economy and not much employment was found for the river folk in the business of guiding.

During the 1930s and '40s, however, many large outfits sprang up along the mainstem Miramichi River. Many of these were founded by businessmen from different cities who had come to the Miramichi to fish and saw the river's potential for the guest camp business. It was then that clubs sprang up under such names as Doctor's Island, Allens, Wilsons, Browns, Jack Sullivan's, Uncle Tom's Cabin and Charlie Wade's Camp.

Charlie Wade was a Justice of the Peace who lived in the Fredericton area. In the early 1930s, he came to the Miramichi to fish, saw it as an outfitter's dream and soon after purchased a cabin near the mouth of the Cains in the community of Howards. Charlie advertised in fishing circles, attended the sportsmen shows in places like New York and Boston, and began booking guests from all corners of the United States. He found a good number of American field sportsmen anxious to visit this part of the northeast where they could canoe our wild rivers and fly-fish for the prestigious Atlantic salmon.

As the business grew, more cabins were built. These were rustic log cabins, nestled in a grove of beautiful pine trees on a bluff overlooking the home salmon pool. Each one was a lodge in its own right with separate cook camp and facilities. Each main lodge had a stone fireplace, rustic dining room and cozy bedrooms. The guides' quarters were nearby in another cabin. Also in the outfit was an office, boathouse, woodshed and icehouses. All were typical of this kind of operation.

In those days, each guest fishing from a canoe needed a guide of his own. Charlie Wade had hired a selected group of local woodsmen, log drivers, canoemen and farmers (all rich in river savvy) to accompany his clients on their fishing expeditions. Charlie's concern for the safety of his guests and their success on the stream was a priority. He hired the mature river-respecting local men. Horseplay was not tolerated. All of Charlie Wade's guides were mild-mannered, humble and generous, with broad Miramichi accents. They knew their place in the operation; once in camp, with the day's fishing completed, the guests were looked after by Charlie himself or his son, Herb, who later took over and still manages the outfit. The Wades were super personalities and all of the guests loved them, but the guides were indeed a great asset to Wade's Camp. As well as being canoemen and guides, these men doubled as makeshift caddies, cooks, storytellers, repairmen and doctors of rare remedies. Above all, they were natural gentlemen and loved the lifestyle as much as the guests themselves did.

These men would be up at daybreak, have a hearty camp breakfast and be ready to head out on the river early in the morning. In the early years, all of the canoes were the 18-foot regular canvas type, made by either the Chestnut Canoe Factory in Fredericton or the Miller Canoe Factory on the Tobique River. As the outfit grew, Wade purchased the larger motor boats, the 22-foot canvas square-stern model with an outboard motor. These larger canoes were used for the spring fishing of black salmon. Many guests returned year after year and warm friendships developed between guest and guide. Some of the guides developed reputations for their successful trips, having guided a famous American. Among these guests were men like General James Doolittle, Admiral Gilette, Charles Goldman (from MGM), Lee Wulff and Stillman Rockefeller.

One story has it that one of the Wade's guides accompanied a famous moose hunter through the woods several miles to the

North Lake. This man wanted a trophy-sized moose and complained bitterly about his guide's choice of a lake. Trying to keep his guest happy, the guide walked him about the hills, getting him lost and returning him to the same lake, the only one in the region. The guest responded, "Ah! A bigger lake and a better lake!" Here, of course, they soon got their moose.

The guides of Charlie Wade—Posing on the grass in front of Wade's Camp are, back row from left to right: Francis Vickers (cook), Earnest Hollier, Stanley Furlong, Lawrence Burke, Melvin Brophy and Patrick Brophy, wearing the light jacket; front row: young Joe Brophy, Peter Colford, George Hennessy (father of Moncton police superintendent George Hennessy), Christopher Brophy, Murdock Burgan, Jack Vickers, Jim Vickers and (uncle) Joe Brophy. Missing from the photo: John Brophy (foreman), Clyde Brophy, Wilson Arbeau, Eldon Curtis, Weldon Peterson and Joseph Brennan. (Author's Collection)

Patrick Brophy, one of the few living members of the group, recalls going to work for Wade as a cook's helper at the age of 13. Later on he was moved from the kitchen when Charlie was short-handed and needed a guide on the spur of the moment.

A swearing-in ceremony at the camp, conducted by Wade and a witness, saw Brophy launch a canoe and set off with a guest. (A registered guide must take an oath to uphold the law, protect the wildlife and work for the general good of the environment.) Years later, Brophy would win canoe races around the province, representing Wade's Camp and Chestnut Canoes Limited.The guides at Wade's Camp became famous in international angling circles, their names often spoken in the banquet halls and dining rooms of the most prestigious fishing clubs in the world, such as the New York Anglers Club and the Theodore Gordon Fishers. Someone wrote:

At night up the steps to Wade's Camp they would come,
Carrying canoe seats, and tackles and salmon each one.
At the top of the hill, to the scales they would go,
Suppose they were weighing a pound heavy or so?
A pat on the back, for a big fish of the day left them
toasting in Boston, "the guides of Charlie Wade."

13

TED WILLIAMS:
FLY FISHERMAN

It was daybreak when Ted Williams and his guide, Roy Curtis, left Williams's summer home at Blackville to drive ten miles upstream to the swinging bridge, their favourite fishing pool. Arriving, they carry their equipment to the shanty on a bluff overlooking the pool and here they busy themselves, assembling fly rods and leaders and choosing flyhook patterns. These men are seventy-ish, khaki-clad and serious.

Williams sits down on a bench in the shanty. He pulls on his chest-high wading boots and throws a pair of suspenders over his shoulders, keeping a glancing eye on his favourite section of the pool. They call it "the cubby." There, only seconds ago, a large salmon broke water. The pool is rippled now by a gentle upriver breeze that sweeps through the shanty and makes the river sparkle in the early morning sunlight.

The men are bronze-tanned from their many days on the river and Williams is some pounds heavier than in the days before his retirement from the Boston Red Sox in 1960. He plucks a flyhook from a fleece patch on his shirt and passes it to me.

"There it is, the great Ingalls butterfly," he booms. "Invented right here in this pool by Maurice Ingalls in the late '50s. It'll work in this kind of water every time."

"Yes, it will, for sure," says Roy Curtis. "We've made some great music with it for sure."

The butterfly is red-butted and Williams has tied it on a number 6 single hook. Its white goat-hair wings are stiff bristles jutting outward from its peacock herl body to make swimming movements when properly retrieved through this kind of water, a presentation that Williams has perfected.

The water is cool and river-smelling as it flows swiftly past. Gulping in the morning stillness, it froths among boulders, setting wallet-sized chunks of foam adrift on the surface. Below the pool, fringed with waving meadow grass, the quiet Miramichi loses itself to the hills.

The July sun is warm and bright as Ted Williams leaves the shanty to wade in at the top of the pool. He makes short false casts as he works his way waist-deep in the current, talking loudly above the din of the water to his friend Roy, still in the shanty rummaging silently about the packsacks.

Curtis has been a guide on the Miramichi River since he left the army in 1939. He can well recall how he first became acquainted with baseball superstar Ted Williams.

"It was in the late '50s," says Roy. "And Ted was an active player with the Red Sox. He was a guest at the Doctor's Island Club in Blackville. I was guiding there. We became friends and when he built his summer place here after he retired from baseball in 1960, he bought a bunch of fishing pools and hired me as his guide and property caretaker."

This was the beginning of a liaison that lasts to this day, recalls Curtis, who through the years has worked for such other camp owners as Kingsbury Brown and the Caldwells. It has also led the Blackville district man into two films with Williams, several appearances on the Red Fisher television show, a book (by John Underwood, entitled (*Fishing the Big Three*)) and a thousand magazine and newspaper articles in such popular publications as *Sports Illustrated}* and *Outdoor Life}*.

"It's been an exciting 25 years," says Roy. "We've had a lot of good times and there have been a lot of rewards."

Through his friendship with Williams, Roy has met such sports celebrities as former boxing champions Jack Sharkey and Gene Tunney, and a host of baseball greats, outdoor writers and sportscasters. These meetings have been sand-wiched in with hunting moose in Newfoundland and wood-cock in Maine, and fishing dozens of rivers throughout the Maritimes. Here on the Miramichi, when the fish are running, they fish eight hours every day. Their relationship is more like two fishing cronies than sport and guide. Each has great respect for the other.

Steven Curtis fishing the Miramichi from a raft. (Author's Collection)

Roy and I watch from the shanty as Williams works his casting line against the breeze. Almost in slow motion, the big left-hander sends the flyhook on a flight across the water as he goes about his strategy, presenting the butterfly to various points in centre stream. His long flowing casts shoot out in giant figure-S patterns, turning the flyhook over for a delicate presentation at near-impossible reaches. At centre stream, a vine-clad cedar abutment projects from the water, the remains of the one-time swinging bridge which gave the pool its name. Cast after cast is made with timed precision as he shoots the tapered flyline against the wind, reaching distances of 80 feet and then 90 feet, perfection each cast.

As the baseball swing of Ted Williams was perfected to form, so goes the fly cast. He works on timing and distance. He has the same dedication, the same zeal and the same ambitious drive for greatness here on the river as when he first arrived in Boston from San Diego in 1937 and was nicknamed "the Kid" by Red Sox owner Tom Yawkey.

"Back then I had set a goal," Williams tells us when he stops fishing to sip tea. "I wanted to be the greatest hitter baseball had ever known. When I left baseball I wanted to be the world's best fly caster. Whether I catch a fish or not, I always enjoy making the perfect cast. The perfect cast is beautiful in itself," he says in his broad American accent.

To be sure, Ted Williams has developed a reputation in fishing circles as one of the world's best fly casters. For him, the art of fly casting and the challenges of psyching the Atlantic salmon into striking the self-tied flyhook are as rewarding as many of his triumphs at the ball park. "It's just as challenging," he says. "If a thing is worth doing and you want to master it, then stay with it until you can do it right. Do it right or don't do it."

And so he goes back to working the pool, presenting a variation of flyhook patterns to the salmon-holding areas. Roy Curtis, who generally fishes along with Ted, today sits on a bench in the shanty and watches. Occasionally he shouts something to Williams, a code or a strategy move unrecognizable to a stranger to the sport. "We've been together so many years, we think as one person," says Roy.

"Years ago, when I first met Ted and he was playin' ball, he would ask me to drive him to different rivers to fish, the Cains or Renous or maybe a river up north. Ted was so popular, I would have to hide the truck in the woods to keep his fans from finding him." Through the years, Roy has learned how to deal with intruders who threaten his friend's privacy. He is always invited into the picture, however, when those film crews or photographers who are accepted by Williams appear. The hero worship has declined somewhat through the years and today, after 30 years, Williams might pass without a glance from the locals. He fits in with the river people, many of whom never followed baseball in the Ted Williams heydays. Many of the intruders are other Americans, seeking the prestige of fishing the Miramichi River with Ted Williams. Even in other parts of the Maritimes the fanfare is greater. When the two went to Newfoundland during the '70s to hunt moose, they had a stopover in Sydney, Nova Scotia. Sydney was a baseball town. When the townsfolk found out Williams was there, they rolled out the red carpet.

"They treated us to free drinks and dinners and literally gave us the keys to the town. Hundreds came downtown to meet Ted and get his autograph," remembers Roy.

But Ted Williams prefers the solitude of a quiet stream or perhaps a woodcock covey. As a man who has spent the greater part of his life in the public eye, he treasures his privacy.

On the Miramichi, Ted and Roy go fishing every morning at daybreak. Travelling in Ted's green pick-up truck, they visit one of his many salmon pools, the choice depending on water conditions. Once at the river, the two veterans examine the designated pool with an air that is gained in this sport by experience alone. They take the scientific approach, testing the water's temperature against its brightness, choosing flyhook patterns that have been tied up by Williams. They kid each other, matching river savvy, sometimes placing small bets on a given flyhook, the speed of a cast or just a salmon's presence in a certain holding spot in the pool. Ted enjoys Roy's easy-going Miramichi style. Roy is a storyteller whose distinctive Miramichi accent spices the humour of his tales.

"I never followed baseball or Ted Williams's career as a ball player," says Roy. "I've always been a fight fan." Consequently, the river guide and the two-time triple-crown winner from the ball park seldom discuss baseball.

"One morning Ted Williams asked me if I would like to meet former heavyweight champion Gene Tunney who was staying at a friend's place in Boiestown," recalls Roy. "I told him, yes, certainly I'd like to meet Tunney. Hell, I'd *walk}* to Boiestown to meet a great sports celebrity like Gene Tunney."

As a guide, though, Roy serves Williams faithfully, carrying lunches and mending equipment. (His wife, Edna, is the cook at the Ted Williams Camp.) He keeps the vehicles and camp property maintained. Many of the repairs are done in the off-season, leaving the angling season free to be spent on the river.

As a fly-fisherman, Ted Williams is all business. He stays on the river patiently hour upon hour. He keeps his eyes trained on the water's surface, watching for the possible movement of a salmon below the surface. He concentrates with a serious-ness that few anglers know. He changes flies and he changes presentation strategy until a salmon strikes and he has gained another victory. Then he plays the fish on his lightweight tackle and guides it into Roy's waiting scoop net; and the fish is released. Then Williams goes back to his original place in the pool and begins to work the area once again. It was this kind of dedication that earned Ted Williams the triple crown of angling in 1978.

When Ted arrived from Florida that spring, he had already hooked and landed 1,000 bonefish and 1,000 tarpon on fly rods and most of these fish, Williams recalls, were released back into the sea. By the autumn of '78, Williams had completed the final leg of his angling triple crown by having hooked and released his 1,000th Atlantic salmon on a fly rod. This was the first such triple crown in the history of fly casting and a feat that may never be surpassed. For Williams, this more private triple crown means as much as the triple crowns he earned with the Red Sox in 1942 and '47.

Like so many celebrities who fly-fish, Ted Williams's devotion to the business of salmon angling and his love for the noble gamefish has led him to become a serious and vocal conservationist, saving this fish from the endangered list. He advocates hook-and-release angling for a cause he describes as being "for the general good of the Atlantic salmon itself as a living species and the fish's value as an important resource to the economy of this province." Williams supports all local conservation groups and is a director of the Miramichi Salmon Association, a group of conservationist/anglers numbering about 500. Williams is frequently photographed setting free a giant salmon after they've done battle.

"Hell, I never kill a fish of any size any more," says Williams, "and certainly not a female. For someone to kill a hen salmon loaded with spawn would be a helluva thing to do. I like the old Lee Wulff line that says an Atlantic salmon is too valuable to be caught only once.

"I consider it a great privilege to be able to fish for the Atlantic salmon, a privilege to catch them for the sport of it and release them unharmed back into the stream," says Williams. "It's the catching rather than the eating that's most valuable."

And so it goes, day in and day out, year after year. The two rivermen travel the gravel back roads to one of Williams's pools in the early morning, fish until noon and return to camp to relax in the heat of the day, only to go fishing again at four in the afternoon and stay on the river until dark.

Williams now uses a special lightweight graphite fly-rod

designed for his summers on the Miramichi. "It offers more of a challenge," Ted says. He uses the weight-forward and double-tapered casting lines and with these he shoots holes in the wind as he reaches across the broad Miramichi to his favourite riff or whirlpool. He is always keeping a sensitive eye on the water's ceiling, looking for the possible indication of salmon movements from deep in the turbulence of the stream. Roy and I watch from the stands as Ted Williams works through the lower end of the swinging bridge pool.

Suddenly there is a screech from the reel and his fly rod is bending double with the strain as a large silver fish flashes its broad sides in the dark amber water and up-ends on the surface. The salmon splashes in a leaping frenzy, fanning its tail, jerking, sending a spray of miniature rainbows into the sun. Hooked!

Roy picks up the scoop and hurries to the shore.

The salmon sets off on a long leaping run downstream, gives a headshake and is free.

"Dammit, that fish got slack line on the last jump, the hook fell out," says Williams. "Ya have to hold 'em high every second, make the rod work."

A fifteen pound Miramichi salmon taken by rod and reel. (Private photo)

Williams returns to his original spot and goes back to casting, throwing his long line across the water, waiting for another strike. Roy wades in behind Ted, and I watch as they fish the pool together.

"I wouldn't trade a day of it," Roy has said. "At what other job could I go fishing every day with someone like Ted Williams, on the better pools of the Miramichi River, and get paid to do it?"

14
MICHAEL WHELAN:
POET FROM RENOUS

Far within the forest scene,
Where the trees forever green
Form a contrast to the beech and birches grey,
Where the snow lies white and deep,
And the song birds seem to sleep,
And cease their sweetest singing all the day.
Where the mighty monstrous moose,
Of limbs both large and loose,
Through the forest sweeps with strides both swift and
strong,
Where the caribou and deer
Swim the brooks so crystal clear,
And the mighty deep Dungarvon rolls along.

Where the black bear has his den,
Far beyond the haunts of men,
And the muskrat, mink and marten swim the stream,
Where the squirrel so light and free,
Swiftly springs from tree to tree,
And the lovely snow-white rabbit sleeps and dreams;
Where the sounds of toil resound
Far across the frozen ground,
And the thousand things that to the woods belong,
Where the saws and axes ring,
And the woodsmen wildly sing,
And the dark and deep Dungarvon sweeps along.

In a lumber camp one day,
While the crew were far away,

And no one there but cook and boss alone,
    A sad tragedy took place,
    And death won another race,
For the young cook swiftly passed to the unknown;
    From the day of long ago,
    Comes this weary tale of woe,
The sad and solemn subject of my song,
    When this young man dropped and died,
    In his youth and manhood's pride,
    Where the dark and deep Dungarvon sweeps along.

    When the crew returned that night,
    What a sad scene met their sight,
There lay the young cook silent, cold and dead,
    Death was in his curling hair,
    In his young face pale and fair,
While his knapsack formed a pillow for his head.
    From the belt about his waist
    All his money was misplaced,
Which made the men suspect some serious wrong,
    Was it murder cold and dread,
    That befell the fair young dead
Where the dark and deep Dungarvon rolls along?

    When they asked the skipper why
    He had made no wild outcry,
He turned away and hid his haughty head;
    "Well, the youngster took so sick,
    And he died so mighty quick,
I hadn't time to think," was all he said;
    A tear was in each eye,
    Each heart it heaved a sigh,
While through each breast the strangest feeling throng;
    When each reverent head was bared,
    As his funeral they prepared,
Where the mighty deep Dungarvon rolls along.

    Fast fell the driven snow,
    While the wild winds they did blow,
Till four feet deep upon the ground it lay,

So that on the burial day
    To the graveyard far away
To bear the corpse impossible was found.
    Then a forest grave was made,
    And in it the cook was laid
While the song birds and the woodsmen ceased their song;
    When the last farewells were said
    O'er the young and lonely dead
Where the dark and deep Dungarvon sweeps along.

    When the crew returned at night
    Their dear comrade still they mourned,
While the shades o' night were falling o'er the hill,
    All that long and fearful night
    All the camp was in affright,
Such fearful whoops and yells the forest fill;
    Pale and ghastly was each face,
    "We shall leave this fearful place,
For this camp unto the demons does belong,
    Ere the dawning of the day
    We will hasten far away
From where the dark Dungarvon rolls along."

    Since that day, so goes the word,
    Fearful sounds have long been heard,
Far round the scene where lies the woodsman's grave,
    Whoops the stoutest hearts to thrill,
    Yells that warmest blood to chill,
Sends terror to the bravest of the brave;
    Till beside the grave did stand,
    God's good man with lifted hand,
And prayed that He those sounds should not prolong
    That those fearful sounds should cease,
    And the region rest in peace
Where the dark and deep Dungarvon sweeps along.

    Since that day the sounds have ceased
    And the region is released
From those most unearthly whoops and screams and yells,
    All around the whooper's sprin

There is heard no evil thing,
And round the Whooper's grave sweet silence dwells
  Be this story false or true,
  I have told it unto you,
As I heard it from the folklore all life long,
  So I hope all strife will cease,
  And our people dwell in peace,
Where the dark and deep Dungarvon sweeps along.

This is Michael Whelan's account of the Dungarvon Whooper, a legendary tale of a lumber camp murder, the woods burial and the mournful shrieks and whoops from the grave that drove everyone from the area, forcing an exorcism to be performed by a local priest. The ballad can be sung to the tune of "Where the Silver Colorado Winds its Way." This is a valued piece of Miramichi folklore and it is generally believed by the river folk that Mike Whelan put it into words better than anyone. Indeed, the literary pursuits of this regional wordsmith have done a great deal for the folklore of Miramichi. Other popular poems were entitled "Farmlands in the Spring," "Leslie Allen," "The Cry of Labour" and "Christmas Bells." Through these poems and many others Mike Whelan has become known as the Miramichi's most significant poet.

Whelan was born in 1858 in the farm community of Grainfield on the Renous River just below where the Dungarvon River makes its confluence. His parents, William and Ellen (Keary) Whelan, were of Irish descent, a working-class couple who operated a family farm with William working the lumber woods. Michael attended the local country schoolhouse but spent much of his youth rambling through the woods and about the farm and river. He had six brothers and two sisters. His brothers moved to the Minnesota area to live and one of his sisters (Margaret) died at the age of three. Michael never married and with his death in May of 1937 the local arm of the family ended.

Poet Whelan was mainly self-educated, remaining a scholar throughout life. He was an extremely well-read man with broad conversational powers. For a time, during his youth, he lived in Western Canada where he taught school on a local license. It is said that Mike Whelan also taught school on the

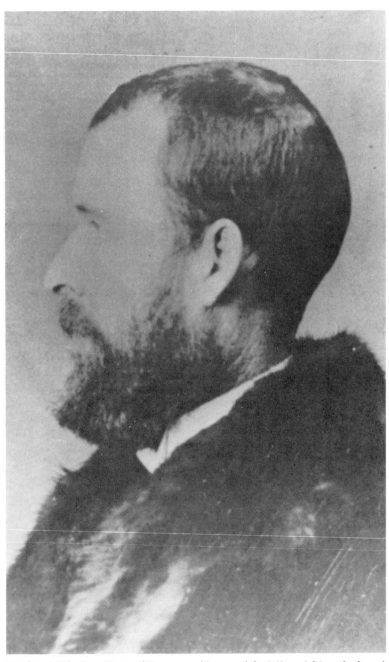

Michael Whelan, Poet of Renous. (*Songs of the Miramichi* anthology)

Miramichi in Grainfield, White Rapids and Cains River. He occasionally hired out as a bookkeeper. His first love, however, was writing poetry and much of his lifetime was spent conjuring accounts of local incident (folklore or legend) of the lumber woods, the farm or perhaps a deceased friend of his native Renous. It was said that Mike Whelan was a deeply religious man and a devout Roman Catholic, a statement often revealed in his works: "It's God's songs that a poet sings."

Mike Whelan was a tall slender figure, slightly stooped, with a greying beard and wearing a long black coat. Bunion-footed, he always wore heavy wool socks in a pair of loose rubbers. He walked wherever he went, his trousers too short by inches—"measured in a snowdrift." University of New Brunswick Professor W.D. Hamilton, in *Miramichi Papers*, described Whelan as "a man three axe handles tall and as wiry as a spring trap." He could be seen almost anywhere along the Miramichi, knocking on doors along the roadway offering a book of verse for a dime or maybe stopping by at a country schoolhouse to read.

Mike Whelan's first poem appeared in 1878, a kind of eulogy upon the death of his friend Bernard McCarthy, Sr. By the turn of the century he had established himself throughout the Miramichi region as "the poet from Renous." Whelan, by his own admission, "sang for the whole people," and his poetry was published in local newspapers and sometimes in the American press; much of his verse carried a message, sometimes religious, sometimes attacking governments on tax rates or appealing for rights for the poor.

> Our government locks up the lumber land
>   That the magnate may rule the sod,
> And guardians over the fisheries stand
>   That were granted us by God;
> Our lumber is taken for half its cost
>   While the merchant profit reaps,
> Our farms are mortgaged away and lost
>   While the farmer works and weeps.
>
> Our workmen toll from dawn till dark
>   In the mills and on the booms,

While the bosses stand like many sharks
　Or shades in the gathering gloom,
Taking two days toll for a half days pay
　And giving poor grub at that
While the workman gropes at the dawn of day
　For his dinner can and hat.

(from "The Cry of Labour")

Then too, his works always revealed his love for the grass-roots Miramichi lifestyle and his boyhood on the Renous. It would appear that Mike Whelan had a chosen selection of intimate friends (among them the priest) but no great love for society in general.

According to Professor Hamilton, "Mike Whelan was a writer of exceedingly serious verse of a religio-patriotic kind—in praise of God, the Catholic Church, Great Britain, Ireland, the United States, Canada, the Miramichi area in general and the Renous in particular." Many of his poems were memorial tributes.

No stone to mark the spot where he reposes,
　No monument above this honor'd dead
No shrine except the sunshine and the roses,
　Above the good, the grey, the gallant head
One of the fathers of confederation
　Who nobly stood and spoke and strove for you,
One of the men who made his land a nation
　He had his faults, but he was tried and true.

O men of Miramichi, have you forgotten
　How this man strove for you in days gone by.

("Peter Mitchell's Grave")

Some of Whelan's books are still in existence in school libraries and archives, with a few most likely valued as keepsakes in the many private homes which Mike Whelan had visited. It is believed that, like any poet, many of the works he had written probably never surfaced at all.

Michael Whelan died a poor man, and was laid to rest at St. Michaels Roman Catholic churchyard in Chatham in an unmarked grave.

Some 44 years later, in a movement spearheaded by Thomas Whelan (no relation, but himself a poet from Chatham) a Michael Whelan Memorial Committee was formed to raise funds to purchase a suitable tombstone for the beloved Renous River poet. Involved in this project were men like Gene Gilles (a great-nephew to Mike Whelan), Miramichi writer Graham Galloway, and Richard Hatfield—then Premier of New Brunswick. Hundreds of fans of the poet made contributions to the cause.

In August of 1981, the gravestone was erected with a brief ceremony for which some 75 persons assembled in the "literary corner" of St. Michaels churchyard. Engraved on the tombstone is a map of that stretch of the Renous River where it is joined by the Dungarvon. This is framed by a bouquet of shamrocks on either side, and across the bottom is inscribed: "Where the deep and dark Dungarvon sweeps along."

15
MILLERTON:
LANDMARKS FROM THE BOOM

Where is the shrill scream of the mill whistle,
The smell of a town built on sawdust and pine shavings?
Where are the logs afloat on the wide river?
Oh sad river,
Sing a song of pain for your children gone,
Oh glory gone.

          - Elizabeth Brewster

 This stanza from the poem "Riversong" could be describing Millerton, a rural community that stretches along the Miramichi estuary, some fifteen miles downstream from Renous and twelve miles below (Indiantown) Quarryville. This is a quiet residential area, a bedroom community for the nearby towns of Newcastle and Chatham. Millerton has a half-dozen 19th-century churches, two schools, two general stores, a post office and a country inn. Also along the highway are many stately old homes from the Victorian or Georgian periods, as well as a number of landmarks that reveal Millerton's glory years as an enterprising lumber town of the 19th century. There are abandoned mill chimneys, a railway bed, decaying wharves and a row of cedar-boom abutments which are strung out at angles across a plate-glass river.

 These century-old landmarks summon visions of another day—workmen hustling about the river booms and the many sawmills, whooping and singing above the din of the saws, their high hobnailed boots, breeches and flannel shirts trademarks of their kind. Only their spirit remains; a spirit that continues to grow thin as their decaying haunts return slowly to the wilderness. The only community employer in Millerton today is the M.F. Esson Company Limited, a road construction/stevedoring firm that employs a number of men.

This community, originally called Miramichi, developed from a farm community to a bustling lumber-mill town in the mid 1800s. John C. Miller, a native of Picton, Ontario, came here in 1869 and established a tanning extract business, using only the bark of hemlock trees. Miller was very successful. Other mills came: the Snowball firm from Chatham put up a mill as did the Beeks, an American group. Another mill, just above the Snowball mill, was Cedar Products Company. The Vanderbeck family also operated a mill as did Father Murdock, a Roman Catholic priest. It was said that at the turn of the century Millerton showed more enterprise and social glamour than the town of Newcastle.

1887 photograph of J.C. Miller's Bark Factory in Millerton. Notice the picket fence along the street. The sled tracks in the foreground leading on to Main Street mark the present Williamstown Highway. Taken from Bett's Windmill Tower. (*J.C. Miller*)

While never incorporated as a village proper, in the later part of the 19th century Millerton could boast such industries as a pulp and paper mill, the bark factory, a tannery, a barrel factory, a plank mill, a gristmill, a wool-carding mill, a shingle mill and a lath mill, as well as the Southwest Boom Company, a logging operation that employed 150 men on the river.

Group of businessmen posing on the Millerton Wharf, having arrived with the riverboat "Mindoo" in the spring of 1887. (J.C. Miller)

The area also offered a good standard of social life as resident dignitaries played host to would-be buyers. Families like the Robinsons (who owned the Boom Company), the Millers, the Vanderbecks and the Hutchisons, the Snowballs and many others hosted buyers from outside who arrived here by riverboat, train, or horse and carriage. These potential customers were treated to posh surroundings and the finest of etiquette, food and entertainment, while the workmen themselves scuffed about in the dust-filled dance halls to the sounds of a scraping fiddle.

Perhaps the most elegant of the homes was the Robinson place. This house still stands today, a spacious old home on an elm-shaded estate, its verandas and bay windows commanding a view of the river. This family had a chauffeur-driven limousine in later years and miles of adjacent farmlands where workmen were employed in the fields.

The Millers' huge home (which also overlooked the river)

was another scene of great social gatherings, offering generous hospitality and becoming one of the leading social centres in the province.

The Robinson House, Millerton, was built by the Robinson family which owned the Southwest Boom Company. This house still stands. (Author's Collection)

Contributions to the area by Mr. Miller were a Presbyterian Church, a skating rink, a community toboggon slide and a wharf. (The remnants of this wharf survive today.) Miller established what is believed to be the first telephone line in the province. A wire attached to the trees along the riverbank extended service from his factory and house to the railway station in Millerton, with another wire running to the house of his friend and business associate R.R. Call in Newcastle, several miles downriver. This telephone system was set up in 1877.

In later years, Miller would drive what may have been the first automobile in New Brunswick. This car was a Winton motor carriage, built in Cleveland, Ohio. It would travel up to speeds of 18 miles an hour "easy, according to conditions of roads and climb a 20 degree grade."

Near the turn of the century, Mr. Miller and R.R. Call built a riverboat and called it the *New Era*. This was used for passenger and freight service and was a part of the transportation swing away from the old stage system in the estuary communities. On holidays, such as Dominion Day, Miller trimmed the large boat with flags and operated free of charge for guests who wished to take a lunch and go on a river trip. Sometimes these excursions would go up the Northwest Miramichi to Red Bank or up the main Southwest to Indiantown. Mr. Miller's generosity and ambitious drive soon encouraged the village to adopt his name: Millertown, and then Millerton.

The Presbyterian Church, Millerton, built by J.C. Miller. (Author's Collection)

General stores sprang up along the main street: the Boom Supply Store, a tavern, two blacksmith shops, a barber shop, a doctor's office, a drugstore, an ice cream parlor and a semi-weekly newspaper called the *Miramichi News*, which was published in Millerton and printed on Millerton-made paper. Subscriptions were a dollar per year. At the turn of the century Millerton had many huge manor houses, stationed at intervals on the slope overlooking the river, each with a large front flower garden and elegant picket fences meeting a board sidewalk. Many homes had windmills. The railway tracks and front street were combined, and a wharf lined the shore where the riverboats came and went frequently, as did the cargo ships.

The Canadian Eastern line of the old Intercolonial Railway built the first railway tracks from Derby Junction through Millerton and on up the river to Quarryville. They ran a mixed train (carrying passengers and freight) from Newcastle to Quarryville, following the river and running directly through the many mill yards in Millerton as well as the bark factory's storage yard. This line, laid in the 1870s, offered new transportation opportunities for the industrialists along this side of the river. The stone quarries upriver at Indiantown would have been the major user of this route.

The quarries prompted Indiantown's name change to Quarryville. This is a small community at the head of the tide where the Renous River makes its confluence with the main river at the foot of the White Rapids. Before the white man came to Miramichi, this had been a tiny Micmac settlement. Legend has it that in ancient times a young Indian maiden sat here on a sandbar, refusing to eat until her lover returned from downstream. She eventually starved herself to death. On the south side of the river, a huge rock, dark and grey, projects from the water: "the Old Squaw." The old-timers claim that in springtime, when the river falls to expose the Old Squaw above the water, bright salmon are in the river.

Further downstream, at Millerton, Barnaby Island offered picnic grounds for river excursions and a place to tie up the raves of logs until they could be distributed to the different mills, having been sorted by means of a colour code at the southwest boom.

While there are many old landmarks remaining in Millerton today, there is little in the way of industry left here from the boom years. Save for the occasional shallow peal of bells from the country churches, the countryside remains silent. The river is silent too. Gone are the shanty songs and the whooping of the rivermen as they shuffle the logs in the great boom; the only sounds on this part of the river now are the mocking chuckles of the wild loons that move about the boom blocks in their stead.

16
NEWCASTLE

1900 photograph of Newcastle, looking over the hill from the present King George Highway. Note the sailing ships. The church at the centre is now in use as a Masonic Lodge Hall. (Miramichi Historical Society)

The town of Newcastle is seated on the banks of the estuary near where the Northwest branch makes its confluence with the main stem of the Miramichi some thirty miles inland and about five miles upstream from Chatham. Incorporated in 1899, the population here varies around 6,000.

Today, Newcastle is a typical eastern town. There are several modern take-out restaurants, a new civic centre and skating rink, shopping malls, motels, restaurants, taverns, a hospital and the county courthouse. There are modern schools both French and English as well as a public library, town hall and theatre, modern recreational facilities, fire and ambulance services and a police patrol. The commons ground in the centre of the business district is called Beaverbrook Town Square. (Newcastle is the boyhood home of Max Aitken, Lord Beaverbrook.)

Presently there are two parks near Newcastle. Beaubears Island, at the river's forks, belongs to Parks Canada and is a national historic site. Wilsons Point (once called Beaubears Point) is the point of land upriver from where the two rivers join and is now a historic gravesite, called the Enclosure Provincial Park.

Points of interest in Newcastle are the Old Manse Library on Mary Street (former home of Lord Beaverbrook), the old courthouse (1829, built by William Murray) on Campbell Street, St. James and St. Johns United Church (also built by Murray in 1829) on King George Highway, the Beaverbrook Town Hall and Theatre (home of the Miramichi Folksong Festival) and the Town Square.

The Town Square, which was given to Lord Beaverbrook by the county in 1959 (in return for his many gifts to us) was immediately embellished by Beaverbrook in the old English fashion. There are six decorative lamps, said to be made from a Russian cannon captured in the Crimean War, which once adorned Admiralty House in London; there are two other lamps reputed to be from the magnificent Dorchester House in Park Lane. Other treasures in the Square are an eighteenth-century sundial from Copt Hall in Essex, garden seats from Syon Park House at Isleworth in Middlesex, and a seventeenth-century gazebo from the great English house of Bramshill.

"The gazebo is often associated with the famous tragedy of Lord Lovel's bride. It is said that on the eve of their wedding, Lovel's bride vanished during a friendly game of hide and seek. The groom never found her and later, maddened with grief, killed himself. Many years after, a mistle-toe bough chest was innocently opened revealing the bridal clothes and bones of the young bride. The bride of Lord Lovel, the grey lady, is said to haunt Bramshill (now a British police academy) to this day.

> Oh sad was her fate—in sportive jest
> She hid from her lord in the old dark chest,
> It closed with a spring—and dreadful doom
> The bride lay clasped in her living tomb."

Also in the Town Square, Beaverbrook installed monuments honouring Peter Mitchell, Newcastle's Father of Confederation, and the pioneer lumbermen and shipbuilders of Miramichi. The Square also offers cobblestone walkways, water fountain (wishing well) and a war memorial which honours the town's sacrifice of soldiers to the two World Wars. The remains of Lord Beaverbrook are also here, with a sandstone monument.

This region has a long history of lumber mills. Since the first English-speaking settlers arrived on the river, through the shipbuilding and lumbering booms of the 1800s and into the 1900s, there have always been several lumber mills here. Today, there are modern mills in and around the town of Newcastle: Northwood Panel Board (a partially employee-owned factory) in Bushville; Burchills plywood mill across the river in Nelson; Andersons sawmill within the town limits; and the region's greatest employer, Miramichi Pulp and Paper, which is said to be the largest pulp and coated-paper mill in the world. The pulp mill is located at the river's forks where the old Sinclair sawmill once stood. Some of the other mills operated in the area over the years have been owned by such families as the Davidsons, Russells, Frasers, Ritchies, O'Briens, Burchills and Hicksons.

While the area has supported some mining and farming through the years, the chief industry has been lumbering—with fishing running a strong second. In fact, in colonial days, the salmon fisheries on the Miramichi figured more strongly in the existence of a settlement than did the other industries. When two Scotsmen, William Davidson and John Cort, arrived in Miramichi in 1765 with a 100,000-acre grant from the

British government, they were not interested so much in this river's abundance of lumber; they were here to establish a salmon fishery. For them, the river was the only means of communications and a source of food supply. To encourage new settlers, promises were made of caribou, moose for the taking and plenty of salmon.

Robert Cooney, wrote in his 1832 *History of New Brunswick and Gaspe}*: "Here about the year 1772 or 73 he [Davidson] and a Mr. Cort, then lately arrived from Aberdeen, set a cross net, with which they annually caught from 14 to 18 hundred tierces [tierce = 300 lb.] of salmon." Indeed, throughout the years, salmon have been served from salt barrels in lumber camps, used for fertilizer by the river's farmers, or traded off to sea captains by white men and Indians alike for kegs of rum. Such exploitation of this natural resource encouraged Benjamin Marston, the district's first sheriff, to write in 1785, "Unless the salmon fishery of this river is attended to [by governments] it will be ruined by the ignorance and avarice of those conceived in it." Today, the resource is still exploited to some degree by poaching, but fish management programs have long since been established and the town of Newcastle remains the official "Atlantic Salmon Centre of the World."

Miramichi} is a Montagnais Indian word meaning "Micmac land." The Micmac Indians were here over 10,000 years before Jacques Cartier sailed across the river's mouth in 1534 and recorded the event in his journal. The Indians themselves were said to have called the river *Lustagoocheehk}*, which meant "little godly river."

The Micmac Indians of the Miramichi were part of an Algonquin tribe that occupied the entire northeast. They were said to have been peaceful, with a good philosophy on life. Before the white man came, the Micmac had done some farming (the growing of indian corn and pumpkins) and they hunted and fished.

It is believed that the Acadians established themselves at Miramichi in the mid 1600s. Certainly this location was part of the Seigneury of Gaspesia, granted to Nicholas Denys in 1648. This grant extended from the Gaspe Peninsula to the Canso Strait. Richard Denys, Nicholas's son, established Fort Fronsac in 1671, building himself a stone house at a point believed to be where the village of Nelson now stands.

There was little activity in Miramichi after Denys' departure (1690) until 1755 when Charles De Boishebert set up an Acadian refugee camp on what is now Beaubears Island. The hardship of the winter of 1756-57 caused hundreds to die on that island and it was eventually vacated.

In the spring of 1765, William Davidson and John Cort sailed into Miramichi. In exchange for their grant of over 100,000 acres from the British government, they were to work the land and establish settlements here. This grant took in what is today the Newcastle area, Beaubears Island, and Nelson, and extended up both rivers (Northwest and Southwest) twelve miles to a point of land on the main river called Elm Tree, where Davidson set up headquarters. The land was to be divided between the two men: two-thirds to Davidson and the balance to Cort. The specific conditions of the grant were the cultivation of 1/3 of this land within ten years, 1/3 more within twenty years and 1/3 within thirty years, plus the settling of one Protestant person for each 200 acres of land and 500 persons within the first four years.

But Davidson was a man obsessed with the idea of harvesting the river's abundance of salmon. He immediately set out to establish trade with Great Britain, some Mediterranean ports and the West Indies. He and Cort established a shipyard on Beaubears Island and Davidson set off for New England where he hired twenty-five skilled workmen and brought them back to the Miramichi to build the badly needed vessels.

By 1773, the crews had finished building New Brunswick's first ship, the 300-ton schooner which Davidson launched and christened *Miramichi}*. They loaded the new vessel with cod and salmon and set sail for the Mediterranean. She was lost somewhere off the coast of Spain and never seen again. During Davidson's time in Miramichi, many of his ships were either lost or shipwrecked.

During the American Revolution, Davidson suffered considerable setbacks when shipping through the Northumberland Strait became almost impossible due to the presence of American privateers. The local Indians made an alliance with the rebel Americans, openly declaring in their favour. Cooney wrote, "They committed the most dangerous outrages:

burned two or more houses; appropriated the peoples [sic] cattle to their own use and plundered what few stores there were; particularly Mr. Cort's from which they took upwards of 700 moose skins and whatever else they considered valuable." John Cort had taken ill and died at Beaubears Point, and Davidson, discouraged with his losses of men and ships, moved to the Saint John River to the already settled town of Maugerville. It was there that he met his wife, Sarah.

But Davidson was a die-hard frontiersman with an ambition to establish himself as a successful merchant in Miramichi. This river's salmon and its virgin timberlands tugged at his soul. He secured a contract to cut masts for the British navy, and in the spring of 1783 he and Sarah returned.

What they found when they returned to Miramichi was a total wilderness. William's old fishing headquarters at Elm Tree had burned to the ground. They had to re-establish shipyards as vessels would be needed to ship masts to the old country. This great need for vessels and the abundance of quality lumber here would lead to the shipbuilding industry that later flourished.

Davidson then re-established his fishery and built a sawmill. The land not being cleared anywhere else, he built a farm on the strawberry marshes. He also cleared some land at the old Acadian settlement site on Beaubears Island and used it for a sheep pasture. The plans for Davidson's settlement had shown Beaubears Point as the town site but, because there were already two log cabins downstream on the marshes that could be used as a jail and courthouse, the town grew in the marsh area where it stands today. (The location of those two log cabins is marked now by the Beaverbrook Town Square.)

New Brunswick separated from Nova Scotia in 1784. Davidson had not lived up to the conditions of his grant, so in 1786 the newly formed government reduced his grant to just 14,400 acres. He lost Beaubears Island and Beaubears Point.

During these years there was migration from Scotland and Ireland to Miramichi. The white population of the Miramichi numbered 233 souls; this census included Neguac and Bay du Vin. Newcastle was a cluster of huts at the Canada Marsh. Among the enterprising young men who arrived were James Fraser and James Thom, two shipbuilders who set up a shipyard on Beaubears Island. By this time, too, William Davidson had been elected to the House of Assembly, representing Northumberland County.

Meanwhile, in the spring of 1785, a Loyalist named Benjamin Marston arrived in Miramichi from Massachusetts. Marston was a Harvard graduate, an upstanding scholar who would hold the position of Northumberland County's first sheriff. He was appointed in June, 1785. It was said that Sheriff Marston had a hard time trying to tolerate the rude and uncultured lifestyle of his raw new country. Marston was a man of strong opinion, sophisticated in his manner and well-spoken. If the people didn't agree with him, he would lash out in sarcastic criticism. He boarded with John Wilson on Wilsons Point (Beaubears). In a letter to his cousin, Edward Winslow, Judge of the Supreme Court, he wrote of the Miramichi and recommended the area for the county seat: "I have not been here long enough to make many observations but this is certainly a very fine country, covered with white clover where ever it is open to the influence of heaven, generally level, easily traversed. To say it was equal to the Saint John, might be looked upon as a species of blasphemy—but this I will dare to pronounce that Miramichi Point and Beaubears Island are superior in situation to Fredericton. A ship of 250 tons from Italy is now lying just to them."

Still Sheriff Marston complained of the coarseness of Miramichiers. He wrote, "Most of the people are illiterate and ignorant and much given to drunkeness [sic]. They want two things, law to keep them in order and gospel, to give them some better information than they seem to have and to civilize their manners which attendance at public worship would tend to promote." Sheriff Marston even complained about William Davidson's fishery, saying that there were far too many nets stretching across the river: "Set nets, which are so extended from each side as to leave the fish very little room to run and at Davidson's are extended fairly quite across the river to the utter exclusion of the poor savage above."

On 17th June in 1790, William Davidson died. He was fifty years old. It was said that Davidson had been laid up since spending a cold February night in a haystack, when he couldn't make it home. He was laid to rest in a grave beneath a huge sandstone slab at Wilsons Point, near the many Acadian graves from the winter of '56. (Davidson's grave is on a point of land overlooking the river junction and Beaubears Island.) William Davidson left his widow and five children to mourn his loss.

As for Sheriff Marston, one story has it that he named the town Newcastle because he always had trouble spelling Miramichi.

By 1792, James Fraser and James Thom exported the first square timber from Miramichi. This was the beginning of the great lumber trade that flourished in the 19th century. During these years, rum was a prominent part of the Miramichi diet. Men took it with them wherever they went. By 1818, it was said that the annual consumption of rum on this river amounted to five gallons for each man, woman and child living here. Sheriff Marston, when he published his charter of the county, denounced the Miramichiers as "a drunken and illiterate lot, all drunk at my expense."

Miramichi historian Dr. Louise Manny wrote, "There were roaring times in Newcastle, when the men came off the drives to spend their winter's earnings in a week's glorious spree. There were riotous summer nights when sailors from the square-rigged ships in port thronged the streets, in drunken hilarity, and eight policemen patrolled the town and were not enough."

By 1825, Newcastle was a thriving town of nearly one thousand inhabitants. There were sawmills, shipyards and wharves as well as stores, churches and schools. Newcastle suffered, however, when the Miramichi Fire swept through the region in October of that year, destroying everything in its path. Newcastle was reduced to just six buildings. Hundreds perished or were left homeless.

By the fall of 1826, the communities were being restored and within a decade of the fire the Miramichi was flourishing on the strength of the lumbering and shipbuilding industries. During the shipbuilding boom, every single foot of riverbank from Beaubears Island to Loggieville seemed to have held a shipyard. Vessels were also shipping out large quantities of the river's lumber. It was said that when newly built ships loaded with timber arrived at their destinations across the sea, both ships and cargo were bought on sight. In 1824, one year before the great fire, the equivalent of 147,000,000 board feet of lumber were shipped from Miramichi. Shipbuilding reached its peak around 1850 and this period produced the best ships in the history of Miramichi. Some of the larger shipbuilders at this time were John Haws, Peter Mitchell, John and Jesse Harding and William Fiddes. In 1857, thirty-six ships were built in Miramichi for overseas buyers alone. The last square-rigger to be built here was constructed at the Harding shipyard in Newcastle, in 1880, by C.C. Watt.

During the shipbuilding and lumbering booms, great rivalries grew between the towns on opposite sides of the river, as companies competed for lumber markets and rights to woodlands. With the rivalries came the "fighting elections" of the 1840s. Two of the major opponents were Alexander Rankin (from the Gilmour/Rankin Company) of Douglastown and Joseph Cunard of Chatham who supported candidates of opposing political beliefs. Joe Cunard was behind John T. Williston of Chatham and Alex Rankin supported J. Ambrose Street, a lawyer from Newcastle. It was said that the quarrelling got so bad at election time that it wasn't safe for a Rankin man to be seen on the Cunard side of the river. There were mob fights and rioting in both towns. The lawless violence reached its peak when a bartender from Newcastle was killed in one such election riot. Local magistrates could not control the mobs and troops were sent to Newcastle from Fredericton to restore order. When the situation deteriorated, elections were done away with completely and government offices were filled by appointment. One New Brunswick magistrate lamented, "There is not, nor ever will be any law in Miramichi."

During the early part of the nineteenth century, many of the buildings in Newcastle were constructed by William Murray, a master builder. He built such landmarks as St. James and St. Johns United Church in Newcastle, St. Pauls Anglican Church in Chatham Head, the old courthouse in Newcastle, the Rankin House in Douglastown and the Roman Catholic Chapel at Moody Point, all of which are still standing and in use today. St. James and St. Johns United Church (then Presbyterian) was Newcastle's first church. Before its construction in 1829, services were held in the county courthouse.

Robert Cooney wrote in 1832:

> The Presbyterian church of Saint James, at New-
> castle is one of the most graceful and elegant specimens
> of architecture in the whole province. Though there is
> in all its arrangements, both within and without, a
> chastity of design and a fidelity of execution; it is in the
> entrance and the spire that the skill of the artist is more
> eminently displayed. The former is a beautiful speci-
> men of the modern, harmonizing with the Grecian
> pillars in alto relievo; and the latter in correct elevation,
> combining a fine union of the Doric, Tuscan and Ionic.

In the mid 1800s, the shipbuilding business declined in
Miramichi and the region turned to exporting deal and other
sawn lumber. Mills owned by the Ritchies, Burchills,
Hicksons, Robinsons and O'Briens were major employers in
the Newcastle area. These owners were part of a rather elite
social circle, with many leading families—the Pollacks,
Gilmours, Rankins, Ritchies and Hutchisons—related by
blood or marriage. At that time there were perhaps ten mills
here.

When the Intercolonial Railway (now CNR) linked Halifax
with Montreal in 1875, it passed through Newcastle. At the
ICR station, a sign was erected naming the stop "Miramichi."
The sign was corrected to "Newcastle" before much time
elapsed.

On May 21, 1881, a log boom on the Northwest Miramichi
River broke. The railway bridge formed a temporary boom
with chains quickly strung out between the piers.

One of the most respected lumbermen in Newcastle was the
honourable Allan Ritchie, who owned a huge sawmill on the
Newcastle waterfront from 1873 to 1927. This mill was lighted
by electricity and operated for 24 hours a day. The Ritchie
House was the first home in Newcastle to have electricity. The
town got electric power in 1901.

In 1899, Newcastle was incorporated as a town and Allen J.
Ritchie, the town's largest employer, was elected mayor by
acclamation.

On November 12, 1914, the Morrissy Bridge was officially

opened by Hon. John Morrissy, then Minister of Public Works for New Brunswick. This steel bridge (still in use) connected Newcastle with Chatham Head, replacing the old ferry that had been in use there.

Since the early days of Miramichi, Newcastle has continued to grow and is now a busy seaport. The town has grown into a beautiful modern town that has gained its wealth through experience in the fishery and lumber trade. The river was dredged to a depth of 8.1 metres (25.5 feet) in 1983. This is the same depth as the St. Lawrence Seaway and allows large vessels to enter our ports to export lumber, ore and paper from the region.

Today the town of Newcastle remains quaint, its people friendly. Aggressiveness in the development of modern facilities by our community leaders keeps the town abreast with the modern world, the way William Davidson in his day strove for equality with his homeland. Newcastle offers a mixture of old and new. The awning-draped, false-fronted stores that join around the old Town Square, tinkling doorbells and friendly calls of "How's she goin'" reveal a strong sense of history: the grass roots. The Victorian houses on Pleasant Street, built for shipbuilders, merchants or lumber kings, are reminders of the past as they stand against time, their towers gleaming above age-old elm trees. At the river, a few shabby packing sheds remain. These once held the Atlantic salmon waiting to be shipped to foreign markets. On the street corners, during summer, aging fishermen, seamen, river guides and American sportsmen gather to swap tales of the current run of majestic salmon. All are reminders of the town's turbulent history and its development through shipbuilding, lumbering and the salmon industry. All are part of our heritage, marking our place in New Brunswick's history.

17
ROBERT RANDOLPH CALL

Robert R. Call was a dominant figure on the Miramichi in the late 1800s. Barrel-chested, with a lean square face and grey beard, Call possessed a rare strength of character that by middle age had fashioned him into a legendary self-made man. In the town of Newcastle he became prominent as a military and community leader.

Call was born in Newcastle in 1837. He was the oldest son (in a family of seven) of Obadiah Call, a man who had moved to the Miramichi River in 1823 from the State of Maine. Robert was educated at the grammar schools in Newcastle and was a loyal member of St. James Presbyterian Church and Northumberland Lodge F and A.M.

On May 21, 1862, he married Annie Neven of Kincardine-shire, Scotland, and they moved into a large house on Hanover Street where they raised a son, Byron, and a daughter, Laura.

A born leader, clear-eyed and resolute, Robert Call had gained the respect of the Miramichi folk—and indeed that of the whole country—before he was out of his twenties. He was made lieutenant of the 2nd Battalion of the Northumberland County Militia in the spring of 1865, and one year later he accepted an appointment as Newcastle's vice-consul agent to the United States. In June of 1867, he was elected chairman of the Northumberland County Alms House Commissioners. The following year, Call organized the Newcastle Field Battery and was immediately appointed captain, a rank which he held for some 30 years.

In 1871, Call and J.C. Miller of Millerton established a riverboat service on the estuary of the Miramichi. They built a side-wheel steamer called the *New Era* which offered passenger and freight service to the many small ports around Newcastle and Chatham. Her home was Call's Wharf in Newcastle.

Lt. Col. Robert Randolph Call, the Newcastle militiaman who worked with J.C. Miller in the riverboat business. (Miramichi Historical Society)

The *New Era* was a success, and two years later Call and Miller had a bigger and better riverboat. This was the huge stern-wheeler called the *Andover*, which they had purchased at a firm in Fredericton and put to a schedule on the Miramichi.

The accounts of the *Andover* need no embroidery and now stand among the fading memories of Miramichi's past like an interval of high adventure and romance. She was a handsome white steamer, 130 feet in length, with her paddle wheel at the stern (in wheelbarrow fashion) and the steering gear underneath. She drew very little water and could travel upriver against the current at a speed of 12 to 15 knots. In July and August the Andover would make moonlight excursions to the downriver ports. Robert Call charged only fifty cents for a regular round-trip ticket from Newcastle to Red Bank.

The riverboat "Andover" owned by J.C. Miller and R.R. Call. She plied the Miramichi for years and took the upriver run to Doaktown. (Public Archives of New Brunswick)

In the spring of 1876, with Call and Miller on board, the *Andover* made a trip up the Main Southwest Miramichi River some 60 miles to the small community of Doaktown, a feat never attempted before or since by such a huge vessel. It was said that through the difficult stretches of river such as the White and the Gray Rapids, local rivermen were called aboard to help the boat's captain find the deepest channels.

One witness wrote, "She was a huge gleaming riverboat, a white plume of smoke puffing from its stacks and the boat itself sitting high above shoreline spruce, the squealing dreary whistle stampeding cattle and horses from riverside pastures with men, women and children crowding on the riverbanks at the various farms waving their handkerchiefs and cheering her on."

Call continued his interest in the riverboat business, later becoming an agent for the Quebec and Gulf ports.

The famous riverboat "Alexandra," used for many years on the Miramichi estuary. (Miramichi Historical Society)

In 1877, Call and J.C. Miller constructed the first known telephone line in New Brunswick. This line ran from Call's residence in Newcastle to Miller's bark factory in Millerton, with another wire running to the Millerton railway station.

By 1881, R.R. Call owned the gas works in Newcastle as well as a coal business which operated on the town's public wharf.

On February 4, 1885, Call was promoted to lieutenant-colonel and in 1894 was named a member of the Board of Pilotage Commissioners for the Miramichi district. He later served as the Board's secretary-treasurer. During these years he also served as ADC on the staff of Lieutenant-Governor Jabez B. Snowball of Chatham. In April of 1897 he was appointed high sheriff of Northumberland County. Lieutenant-Colonel Call retired from public life in 1898.

R.R. Call had travelled widely in Canada and in Europe. He thrived on adventure and had a love for the military. On the Northwest Miramichi River he owned and operated a fishing lodge near a stretch known as Call's Pool where he hosted fishing parties of distinguished guests from the United States. Among these were such men as congressman John S. Adams, Esq. of New York; a native of Douglastown, William Crawford; Dr. Crawford of New York; and Michael Adams, ex-surveyor general of New Brunswick.

A long retirement was not for Call, however: he died in December of 1903. It was said that he collapsed in the snow after stepping from his sleigh at Newcastle's railway station, on his way to attend the funeral of his friend, John S. Fleming.

Millerton-born Hedley Parker, then a journalist in New York, wrote, "Men early recognized in [Call] that personal magnetism that tends to the solution of problems and turned instinctively to him in emergencies." Indeed, the river folk respected him as an authority and a just man. In the words of Rev. William Aitken, "We may truly say that in the majority of homes on the Miramichi, his name was a household word."

18
MAX AITKEN:
LORD BEAVERBROOK

When Max Aitken arrived in Newcastle in the spring of 1880 he was just ten months old. He had been born in Maple, Ontario, on May 25th, 1879; he was the son of Rev. William Aitken, and the sixth in a family of ten children. The Aitkens were of Scottish ancestry and Max's father, a Presbyterian minister, had come to the Miramichi to preach at St. James Church.

The Aitkens moved into the manse at 225 Mary Street, a Victorian-style house just three years old. It had been built as a private home for a shipbuilder and merchant, William Watt, but was purchased by the congregation in 1879. Rev. Aitken was the first clergyman to occupy the house and it was here that Max lived until he was eighteen years old.

Max Aitken was often described as a loner, full of mischief and maybe a trifle rebellious against the strict, orderly household at the Presbyterian manse. His father, Rev. William Aitken, was a tall scholarly man with a long white beard, a patriarch who perhaps could have gone to a big city and occupied a higher position with a larger congregation. But he loved the Miramichi and, with a fine collection of books, he and his large family found contentment in Newcastle.

Young Max commenced his education at Harkins Academy on Prince William Street. He was mischievious, one of the "bad boys" of the class. His teacher had put him in a front seat "to keep an eye on him." Max was only a fair student with his strength in mathematics. He did like to read, however, and his favourite authors were Scott, Stevenson and perhaps Thackeray. Of Dickens, years later he wrote, "I could not abide that public favourite in youth, nor in old age."

The Manse, Lord Beaverbrook's boyhood home, with the Rev. William Aitken and his young family on the steps. The Manse is now a public library. (Miramichi Historical Society)

Max was not unlike a Dickensian character himself, with his lively imagination and extreme restlessness. The principal at Harkins Academy (1884-1892), Dr. Philip Cox, wrote, "He impressed me as being an absent-minded boy, as if he were always thinking of something beyond the subjects of the classroom or perhaps of the next prank he could carry out with success." Max surprised the teachers, however, by submitting a brilliant essay on Warren Hastings before he left school in the tenth grade. Many years later he wrote, "It was a good form of education, surpassing that given at public schools in England. If I had the education of my sons to supervise over again I would not send them to the English public schools. I believe they would get a better preparation for life at Harkins Academy in Newcastle."

As a boy, Max Aitken was always doing odd jobs to make a few dollars. By the age of eight he had organized an egg market. Lord Castlerosse told the story that Max once received a sudden call for an unexpected number of fresh eggs and he ran short. In the kitchen at the manse there was a store belonging to the household. They would not be wanted, but his mother was out. Max made a quick decision: he borrowed the family eggs. The next day he met his client.

"Max," she asked, "were those eggs fresh?"

"Why, weren't they?" countered Max in the most innocent tone of voice.

"Well," continued his victim, "they were the first fresh-laid eggs I have ever seen arrive in the world hard-boiled."

"Ah!" said little Max. "I was frightened that that thunderstorm we had yesterday would affect the hens!"

The town of Newcastle was a small town back in the 1880s when Max Aitken was growing up here. In *My Early Life*, he described the many small farmhouses that stood in clearings made in the overwhelming mass of dark forest. Out here, he wrote, a stranger would be hopelessly lost before he had gone far from the nearest pasture or house. In those days, Aitken recalled, there was always plenty of game. "The bear could be shot by the sportsman, the wild partridge came down to feed of the crops, and the great moose has been known to pay a visit at night and stamp with his mighty hoofs on a garden in the main street of Newcastle."

Behind the manse, across the back road, there was a pasture where Max milked the cow daily. Sometimes he would steal off to the barn and hide away, reading Scott. He had to share such household chores as carrying in the evening's wood and drawing the well water. He also had a newspaper route. At church on Sundays he sometimes refused to sit in the family pew, but wandered among the "non-believers" in the gallery, where he sat with a black friend.

Max was eleven years old when the Women's Auxiliary installed a new pipe organ in the church, and his father hired him at 25 cents a week to pump the bellows. During church sevices, young Max sheltered behind a screen where he was free to read. He detested the job on choir practice nights, when the light was dim and the church was cold. He said he had the advantage over members of the choir, though, "of vigorous exercise in pumping up-down-up-down, keeping a steady rhythm lest the organ notes varied in tone through excessive pressure."

On a dull and dreary Sunday evening in mid winter, after a sleepless night, young Max "fell into slumber, dreaming of pumpkin pie." He was not awakened by the voice of his father announcing the hymn, "A Few More Years Shall Roll."

The organ gave only silence. When Mr. John Brander awakened him, Max grasped the pump handle and in a desperate attempt to get the organ going supplied too much energy, so that the organ released an awful "wailing noise, as though a restless spirit was trying to escape from the graveyard."

For that he "got the sack." The next Sunday his father made him sit in the manse pew, "in the front line facing the congregation." His brother took his place behind the screen at the pump. "I had lost my first job and the salary of 25 cents a week.

Max Aitken had been described as "the boy with the big head." Certainly he had a broad innocent smile and in his young days a freckled nose which gave him a happy-go-lucky appearance. In summertime he would roam the strawberry marshes barefooted. For months he wouldn't know the feel of shoes on his feet. One autumn, when he put on his boots for the first time, a passing mowing machine that was being pulled behind a cart caught his attention. He grabbed hold of the pole, meaning to run along with it.

"My boots, to which I was not yet accustomed, brought me down in the road and the wheel of the mowing machine passed over my head." Max was carried away. He remembered nothing of what happened after that. When he woke up in a few days, he was conscious that there had been an accident but was not clear about what had happened.

But he did know one thing. "When I took hold of the pole of that mowing machine I was a stupid boy who showed no remarkable qualities whatever. But when I returned to consciousness after the accident, I was a clever boy." He always felt that the crack which the wheel gave to his skull gave the brain room to expand, which it needed. "Doctors can make what they like of the accident. I have made a lot of it."

At the age of thirteen, Aitken produced a newspaper. It was called the *Leader* and cost a cent. He set his own type and drove the press by hand. Then he sold the paper in the streets, his spaniel, Tasso, following at his side. The newspaper ended because of a delay in publication. It should have been published on Sunday morning, but Max was still labouring to produce it in the early hours of Sunday morning. The whole enterprise was broken up by his father who appeared at the office at two a.m., shocked by the desecration of the Sabbath. By this time, though, Max was selling and collecting for the *Provincial and Daily Sun* and a correspondent for the *Saint John Sun*.

When Tasso died, he buried the dog "in the manse garden beneath a hedge of spruce trees." Forty years or so later, Aitken still remembered Tasso and when he bought a little white mongrel at his gate for five shillings, he gave him the same name. The little dog quickly won his affection, and everywhere he travelled, the second Tasso kept him company.

One day, waiting for the London train to Southampton, he was approached by a stranger whose obvious accent proclaimed him an American.

"Will you sell me your dog?" he asked Beaverbrook.

"Yes, indeed."

"I'll take him," said the American. "What price?"

"One million dollars," answered Beaverbrook.

When Max Aitken was sixteen years old, he went to Dalhousie University in Halifax to write his entrance papers. He had borrowed the money for this from Edward Sinclair, a friend in Newcastle. At Dalhousie the entrance papers were going well until the third day when he was given the Greek and Latin. Aitken "took hostility to these dead languages" and the papers were returned to the examiner with declaration that "a university career involved unnecessary and useless labour in futile education pursuits." His college career ended. Years later, after Edward Sinclair's death, Beaverbrook repaid the debt by endowing the Edward Sinclair Arena in Newcastle.

Back from Halifax, Aitken went into law, studying with Richard (R.B.) Bennett at the law office of L.J. Tweedie in Chatham. He had met Bennett on a riverboat (the *Miramichi*) which was plying between Douglastown and Newcastle. Aitken had been impressed with Bennett, a well-dressed, tall, self-deprecating man who was polite and intellectually honest. Aitken wrote, "In that short journey of four or five miles I formed a strong friendship that lasted for more than fifty years."

Legal training in New Brunswick was on the apprenticeship basis instead of through a law school. Mr. Tweedie wrote, "After Aitken had been in my office for a month, I was not sure whether he was working for me or I for him." Aitken stayed in Chatham for a year and a half. Some of his cronies in those early years were Bill Corbett, Hubert Sinclair and Jack Sweet. Later he went to study law in Saint John and from there he went to Halifax and then Montreal.

But he would always love the Miramichi River and Newcastle. He wrote, "Newcastle always seemed to be 'home' to me. No matter how strongly business affairs in Halifax and elsewhere called me, the return to the town on the rive, thrills me with happy emotions and feelings of deep affection for the people."

On 25th May, 1900, Aitken turned 21: he celebrated by spending three days fishing with friends in Nova Scotia. At this point in time Aitken felt he had been wasting his life. On this trip, while listening to an acquaintance brag about his business triumphs, he decided, "Now I'm going to make some money quickly. I'm going to sell what makes money." He took to financing at the right moment.

He sold bonds and it was said that Aitken's word was literally his bond. He was a man of financial integrity. No one ever lost a penny through investing in his companies. He created a series of individual complexes which now stand as monuments of his genius. He sold insurance and he bought and sold trust companies, railways, gas companies and electric-light companies as far off as South America. Max Aitken had become a prominent financier and his advice in this field was highly valued. He assisted in important bank and steel industry mergers as well as in the mergers of thirteen cement companies. Max Aitken turned himself from a poor boy into a millionaire.

In 1906, Aitken married Gladys Drury. She was a tall blonde with large green eyes, the daughter of General Charles Drury, a noted military man of that day. The Aitkens honeymooned in New York. Gladys was slightly above Max socially and was a great asset to him. Their daughter, Janet, was born in Halifax in 1908, and in 1910 their son, Max, was born in Montreal. It was around this time that the Aitken family moved to England.

In England, Aitken found that some of his associates had come from his Canadian home. Andrew Bonar Law, a future prime minister of Great Britain, was the son of a Presbyterian minister who had been at the nearby parish of Richibucto. James Dunn had come from a few miles to the north of Newcastle.

Dunn's mother, formerly of Newcastle, had been widowed at twenty-five and worked as the local agent of the Western Union Company to support herself and her son. He became Sir James Dunn, whose name played so large a part in Canadian industrial history. He had made a fortune before the First World War and died in 1956 leaving an estate worth many millions.

Years after the death of his wife, Gladys, Beaverbrook married his long-time family friend, the widow of Sir James Dunn. (Lady Dunn now lives in St. Andrews, New Brunswick.) Beaverbrook wrote of the marriage, "I have found a woman who loves me not for my money but for myself alone."

And of course R.B. Bennett, former prime minister of Canada, was also living in England. Here at home Aitken had made a fortune in business; in Britain he would venture into politics and journalism.

It was said that Aitken's advice in politics was as highly valued as in finance. New challenges along the way would bring him to become an important newspaper proprietor and then a statesman. Historian, art lover, and indeed a character, in the words of A.J.P. Taylor (honorary director of the Beaverbrook Library), "he was a most extraordinary man. There are more anecdotes about him than about any other figure of his time except possibly Churchill."

Max Aitken became a private secretary to Andrew Bonar Law who became prime minister of England under his guidance. By late 1910, Aitken had been elected himself to the British House of Commons. In 1911, he was knighted and by 1916 had been made a baronet. In 1917, he was raised to the peerage. When Max Aitken was asked to choose a title, on the advice of Rudyard Kipling he took the name Beaverbrook after the tiny community on the Miramichi. "The Beaver" was the nickname often given to him by the public on both continents.

In 1916, Beaverbrook purchased the *Daily Mail* and commenced to build his career in the newspaper business. This was a newspaper that catered to the lower classes. He eventually owned a whole network of papers among which were the *Daily Express* (a family newspaper), the *Times*, the *Evening Standard* (which catered to the upper classes) and the *Scottish Daily Express*. All of the newspapers had a wide circulation because of Beaverbrook's ability to carry topics for all classes and age groups in society. Beaverbrook seldom appeared at a newspaper office but communicated with his editors by phone.

It has been said that Beaverbrook used his newspapers for political influence but this is not so. While it is true that Beaverbrook enjoyed the power that newspapers gave him, he had been into politics as a Member of Parliament long before he had been involved with newspapers. In fact, Beaverbrook was something of a radical in the Conservative party. He used the newspapers to speak out against the government, giving his own views as a free-thinking man. Beaverbrook's belief in Irish freedom was inconsistent with government policy. On topics such as the intervention in Russia in 1919, Lloyd George's projected war with Turkey in 1922, and free-spending tactics for recovery during the Great Depression, Beaverbrook took a stand contrary to the government's. He had been appointed Minister of Information in World War I and he always believed in a free-trading empire, thinking that perhaps the Dominions could strengthen the mother country in times of war and benefits from the unity would make them prosper. This Empire crusade, he realized before his death, was a fantasy.

When World II broke out, Sir Winston Churchill appointed Lord Beaverbrook Minister of Aircraft Production because of his reputation for "improvisation and drive." In the event of a German invasion, some claimed, Churchill would have set up a dictatorship of Beven, Beaverbrook and himself. Beaverbrook himself wanted to be known simply as a journalist and that is what he called himself on his passport.

From 1941 to 1942, Beaverbrook was Minister of Supply and from 1943 to 1945 Lord Privy Seal. He left politics in 1945 and retired to his newspaper empire.

Lord Beaverbrook stops to chat with youngsters on one of his many trips home from Britain. (Author's Collection)

Lord Beaverbrook loved Canada and especially his home, Newcastle. He returned almost every year for a visit, attending convocations at the University of New Brunswick and driving the winding river road along the Miramichi to Newcastle, where he had many historical projects in progress. He had planned to retire here someday, to a sandstone house called the McTavish Farm. When he was in Newcastle, he smiled and greeted everyone he met as though they were his long-time friends. He was always very generous, establishing university scholarships for promising young students. He gave to Newcastle the Sinclair Arena (a beautiful skating rink that has since burned down) and the Beaverbrook Theatre and Town Hall. In 1953, Lord Beaverbrook purchased the Old Manse (his boyhood home) from St. James and St. Johns United Church and donated it to the town of Newcastle to be used as a public library. With the library, Beaverbrook gave more than 10,000 books in many different languages. (Today the Old Manse Library has an estimated 30,000 books as well as clippings, documents and other resources.) Beaverbrook was also instrumental in the restoration of the old gravesite at Beaubears Point, now the Enclosure Provincial Park. He also donated church organs, chimes and bells. During the mid 1950s, he assisted Dr. Louise Manny (a personal friend and librarian at the Old Manse) with her collection of Miramichi folksongs, which would be known as the Beaverbrook Collection. (Dr. Manny founded the Miramichi Folksong Festival which is held in the Town Hall in Newcastle each August.)

In return, in 1959, the County of Northumberland presented Lord Beaverbrook with the Town Square. Beaverbrook then furnished the Square with eighteenth-century lamps, a gazebo, and monuments to Peter Mitchell, Newcastle's Father of Confederation, and to the pioneer lumbermen and shipbuilders of Miramichi.

When Lord Beaverbrook was an old man occupied at a desk, he was approached by Sir Winston Churchill.

"What are you doing?" Churchill asked.

"Writing," Beaverbrook replied.

"What do you write about?"

"Me."

"A good subject," said Churchill. "I have been writing about me for fifty years and with excellent results."

"There's not much time left to us. We've both done our threescore years and ten," said Beaverbrook and then he sang:

A few more years shall roll,
A few more seasons come,
And we shall be with those that rest
Asleep within the tomb.

When Lord Beaverbrook died in England in 1964, his ashes were returned to Newcastle and were placed by Lady Beaverbrook in the sandstone base of Oscar Nemon's bust of him which stands in Newcastle's Town Square. The ceremony was attended by dignitaries from around the world.

"I am content," he wrote in 1956, "for I have been blessed far beyond my deserts and my last home will be where my heart has always been."

19
DR. LOUISE MANNY

One of the ladies most respected and loved by the people of the Miramichi River was Louise Manny of Newcastle. She was a noted historian, author, humanitarian, and in general a distinguished lady, highly intelligent with a broad range of interests.

Indeed, Dr. Louise Manny's contribution to the heritage and cultural life of the Miramichi may never be surpassed. She was founder of the Miramichi Historical Society as well as the Miramichi Art Club. She was active in the New Brunswick Historical Society and a committee member of the New Brunswick Museum. She served on the advisory board of the Historic Sites Protection Committee and on the Provincial Centennial Committee. She also held membership in the North East Folklore Society of Maine.

But Dr. Manny is perhaps best remembered by the Miramichi people for her role as founder of the Miramichi Folksong Festival in 1957. A week-long singing celebration, held each August in the Beaverbrook Theatre/Town Hall in Newcastle, the folksong festival is the longest running of its kind in the country. The festival was organized with the support of Lord Beaverbrook and directed by Dr. Manny until her death in 1970.

Louise Manny was not born on the Miramichi River but in Maine, in a community called Gilead. She was the daughter of Charles and Minette Manny who were descendents of the early Dutch settlers of New York. The Mannys moved in 1893 to Newcastle, where Charles had found employment with R. Corry Clark in the spoolwood business. Louise was then three years old.

She was educated at Newcastle's St. Marys Academy and

Dr. Louise Manny, Newcastle's best-known historian, was founder of the Miramichi Folksong Festival in 1958. (*Author's Collection*)

Harkins Academy before going to the Halifax Ladies College. From Halifax she advanced to the Ursuline Convent in Quebec City and eventually graduated from McGill University in 1913 with a Bachelor of Arts, receiving honours in both English and French.

Manny then returned to Halifax where she taught for a while before returning to Newcastle because of her father's failing health. She took a job as a secretary with the same spoolwood firm that had employed her father.

A long-time personal friend of Lord Beaverbrook, Manny was given the job as librarian at the Old Manse Library, when Beaverbrook purchased the manse from the United Church and donated it to the county as a public library. She served there from 1953 to 1967.

Dr. Manny always worked closely with Lord Beaverbrook on his many historical projects of Miramichi. The restoration of the Enclosure Provincial Park was undertaken by Beaverbrook with Manny as an assistant. Lord Beaverbrook entrusted to her the task of making sure that none of the park's natural beauty was lost in the restoration. It was said that workmen at the park wouldn't so much as cut down a bush or pick a wildflower without asking Dr. Manny. She also saw that Lord Beaverbrook's wishes concerning the refurbishing of the Town Square were carried out.

In 1968, Louise Manny and her friend Dr. James Reginald Wilson, a university professor at Douglass College, New Jersey, assembled a 330-page anthology entitled *Songs of Miramichi}*: a collection of 101 Miramichi folksongs.

At the folksong festivals in those early years, Manny acted as master of ceremonies, introducing the songwriters and singers who came from all regions of the river to perform at the Beaverbrook Theatre. She also acted as disc jockey for her own radio show (on CKMR) which featured folk music.

As a community worker, she served as secretary of the Miramichi Hospital Board of Trustees. She was a director of the Children's Aid Society and was active in the Canadian Red Cross Society. She was a valuable source of information on antiques, folklore, old books, glassware and art.

Dr. Manny loved sports and was active in tennis, badminton and swimming. In the 1930s, she won a number of

Maritime tennis titles for double play.

She was also a poet.

She received honorary doctorate degrees from both the University of New Brunswick and St. Thomas University.

The lieutenant-governor of New Brunswick, J.B. McNair, presented Dr. Manny with an award from the American Association for State and Local History.

In 1967, at Expo in Montreal, Dr. Manny was presented with the Centennial Award of the National Council of Jewish Women for outstanding service to Canadian cultural life. She was one of eleven women in Canada to receive this honour.

In 1969, a mountain in a remote wilderness some forty-five miles northwest of Newcastle was named Manny Mountain in her honour by the province of New Brunswick.

Dr. Manny died on August 17, 1970. Her remains were buried in the Miramichi Cemetery, Newcastle. On August 3rd, 1987, a monument honouring Louise Manny was unveiled in the Town Square.

20
THE BEAVERBROOK COLLECTION

It's almost forty years since Lord Beaverbrook said to Newcastle librarian, Louise Manny, "Why don't you go out and collect New Brunswick folksongs? I'll send you a fine recording machine."

"Folksongs?" said Dr. Manny, "I don't believe there are any—not nowadays at least—unless someone can remember 'Peter Emberley' which your brother Traven used to sing."

"Nonsense! Of course they have folksongs. Why, when I was a boy they had a song about the Jones boys—

The Jones boys! They built a mill
On the side of a hill,
And they worked all night,
And they worked all day,
But they couldn't make that gosh-darned
Sawmill pay.

Now that's a genuine folksong," said Beaverbrook.

It was then that Dr. Manny and a friend, Bessie Crocker, began their search through the farms and lumberwoods of the Miramichi's remotest reaches in a quest for the homespun poems and folk ballads that would make up the Beaverbrook Collection.

Among the songs found by Manny and Crocker were the grass-roots songs of the Miramichi working folk. Many of these had been written by local river people, preserved in memory and passed on by word of mouth for generations. The English, French and Micmac cultures contributed volumes of river songs, many of which were later published in an anthology by Dr. Manny and Reg Wilson entitled *Songs of Miramichi*.

These songs were written largely from the inspiration of tragedies, comedies, folklore and legend in this part of the northeast. There were songs of the sea, shipbuilding songs and songs of the lumberwoods. There were the shanty songs and the log drive songs as well as farm songs, love songs and songs of superstitions, many of which were related to drinking sprees, murders, hangings, ghosts and forerunners. The Miramichier had a song for just about everything he did, from working at the sawmill to milking a cow or even picking blueberries. Many of these ballads begin, "Come all ye jolly lumbermen [or farmers, or sailors] and listen unto me."

Most of the songs in the collection were sung as solos and without musical accompaniment. Only the occasional toe-tap of the singer helped determine the intended tempo or meter. The tunes to which these ballads were sung are closely related in that there are no difficult passages or pitches to create problems for the singer. Many of the tunes were believed to have been brought here generations ago from the old country. A common practice was to recite the last few words or even the last stanza, adding a "Whoopee" at the end to indicate that the song had ended. This also cleared the air for the next singer.

In the days before radio, a common social event on the Miramichi was "the singing bee." This would take place in a local farmhouse when two or three neighbours got together to sing. Each man sang different songs from memory, in rotation, until only the winner was left with a song to sing. Such an event could last for days. It is said that the Miramichi folksong was written by Miramichiers about other Miramichiers, to be sung to Miramichiers.

In the old days, every community had a fiddler. This man would go around from house to house playing for parties and social gatherings. Few Miramichi fiddlers could read music and their tunes were either made up by the fiddlers themselves or learned by ear and the grapevine from someone who had heard another fiddler, perhaps in another settlement. "They say that Jack the Fiddler has learned another new tune. He heard it from Dan's girls who got it from McGilvery."

As a result of this kind of musical communication, many songs changed in both tune and lyrics. Sometimes, the tune was changed to suit the fiddler's capabilities. No one really cared, because it was *music* and few knew a difficult scale from an easy one. These old fiddlers knew very few tunes and throughout the years they continued to play their own favourites until a certain tune and its player were identified as one. A tune might become known as "Flora's Tune," or "The Jack Burke Tune," or whatever.

When the fiddler started to play, someone in the audience whooped. The Miramichi whoop was a half-yodel release of emotions that seemed to lift others to their feet. The fiddle inspired the whoop and there were good whoopers and bad. It was said that Blackville's Max Schofield could let out a whoop that would bring a dead man to his feet. The Miramichi became known for its whoopers: we've had a ghost, an express train and a tavern that carried the name.

If someone wanted to have a party and they were unable to get a fiddler, they would have to settle for the next best thing: a good diddler. There was always a man in the community who had a reputation for his diddling talent. Some were better than the fiddlers themselves. "Whoop and drive 'er" would be the shout from the floor to start the diddler. He would sit in a chair, clap hands, tramp his feet or maybe even beat two spoons together and diddle with only the occasional drink of rum to moisten his vocal organs. Most often such a music man would render jigs and hornpipes in a jazz fashion, with someone else calling the dance.

It was said that Joe Smith, a woodsman-guide who was also a poet and songwriter, could make a sound deep in his throat that resembled a church organ. Witnesses claimed that if Big Joe was humming in another room not even a musician would know his sounds from real music. As a result of this rare talent, he was often invited to perform at social gatherings. Whenever he and Tom Curtis got together at socials, Joe would "play" the organ and Tom would sing.

Among the most popular of the woodsmen's songs are the "Dungarvon Whooper" and "Leslie Allen," both written by Michael Whelan, the poet from Renous, and both inspired by woods tragedies. "Peter Emberley" is another Miramichi ballad which deals with a lumber-woods death. This song was written by John Calhoun, a lumberman and farmer from

Parkers Ridge. Calhoun was known to have an expert handling of rhythm and he was a good philosopher. His song is believed to have travelled to every lumber camp in North America, put to the melody of an old Irish ballad.

The people of Miramichi are grateful to Lord Beaverbrook for conceiving the idea of a folksong collection, and to Dr. Manny and Bessie Crocker who found much of this music which otherwise might have been lost forever. We are also grateful to a host of folksingers, writers and fiddlers who came forward with songs and tunes to revive this part of our heritage.

In 1958, Dr. Louise Manny founded the Miramichi Folksong Festival. This is an annual three-day sing-along featuring the traditional river songs and music. Dr. Manny directed the festival for many years. It is now under the direction of Mrs. Susan Butler, a local singer and composer.

Other songs heard at the festival feature names like "Duffy's Hotel," "The Miramichi Fire," "The Steamer Alexander," "Eight-Pound Bass" and "The Home Brew Song," all part of the Beaverbrook Collection.

21

NELSON-MIRAMICHI
AND BEAUBEARS ISLAND

What cause you have to bless the giver
  The broad, majestic Miramichi,
Dear Nelson, nestled by the river
  For gracious gifts to thee.
 Sweet village resting by the river
  That flows forever to the sea,
While shadows on thy bosom quiver,
  I sing this song to thee.

                    - Michael Whelan, 1914

Nelson is a charming old village which is located on the south side of the river opposite Newcastle. Its location makes the major centres of Newcastle and Chatham very accessible to its residents. The main street winds along the river's edge, commencing at Chatham Head which is on the south end of the Morrissy Bridge and extending upstream to points beyond the upper end of Beaubears Island, into the more rural communities of Chelmsford and McKinleyville, across the river from Derby.

This village has a population of about 1,500 and was officially incorporated in 1967 as Nelson-Miramichi, with Mr. Byron Goodin as the first mayor. Since that time, Nelson has obtained a new civic centre and fire hall (with a total of five firetrucks and 30 volunteer firefighters), village offices and a recreation centre as well as an outdoor skating rink. Businesses in the village include Beaubears Co-Operative Store, Beaubears Credit Union, Papa Joe's Store and Shear Magic Beauty Salon as well as the Governor's Mansion Country Inn and Doucet's Bed and Breakfast. The village also has three churches, schoolhouses, a post office and a senior-citizens' complex. Industry in the village includes Alex Flett Construction, the Miramichi Pulp and Paper Inc. sawmill, Burchill's plywood mill and Newco Enterprises Limited. While there are modern subdivisions within the boundaries of Nelson, and many modern houses, this community has a wealth of residences that are among the oldest in the province.

The oldest existing house on the river is said to be that of John Saunders, which was built at the mouth of the Barnaby River in 1804. Other historic houses in Nelson include the Percival House (1825), the Flett House (1830), the George Burchill House (1857) and the O'Brien House (1860).

The village of Nelson is directly behind Beaubears Island, across the river from Wilsons Point (the Enclosure Provincial Park) where the Northwest Miramichi flows into the main stem. The Micmac Indians called this area *Niktawak*, which means "at the river's forks." The name *Kwoomenigook* was given to the island, meaning "beautiful island of the pines." Today, Beaubears Island (now a national park and historic site) is a sanctuary of beautiful tall pine trees. These ancient trees are believed to be the only stand of this kind left on the river, preserved as a reminder of the virgin forest that fell to the shipmast industry.

Nelson and Beaubears Island are believed to be the first areas of the Miramichi to be settled by the white man. In the words of Earl English, a Nelson historian, "The history of Nelson and the history of Beaubears Island are one in the same." They were part of the Seigneury of Gaspesia, granted to French governor Nicholas Denys in 1648. Denys had a trading establishment in Miramichi, probably at Nelson's location. His grant extended from the Gaspe Peninsula to the Canso Strait. Richard Denys, Sieur De Fronsac, Nicholas's son, established Fort Fronsac in 1671, building himself a stone house near Flett's Cove in Nelson.

Nicholas Denys wrote of the salmon in Miramichi: "So great a quantity of them enters into this river that at night one is unable to sleep so great is the noise they make in falling upon the water after having thrown or darted themselves into the air."

In 1688, Richard Denys wrote:

I have there a fort built of wood with four bastions, where I have eight pieces of cannon, two of brass, four pounders, and two of iron, four pounders, and four other pieces of iron, eight pounders, and good muskets, with twelve men resident winter and summer, and a clerk who is in command and two men for the fishing of cod.

This year there are eighty wigwams of Indians who are more than five hundred persons counting the women and children. I have a store house from which the Indians and French get their supplies. There are three residents.

According to Earl English's book, *Nelson and Its Neighbours*, Richard Denys left the river in 1691, going to Quebec from where he sailed for France on the *Francois Xaviar*. He perished on the trip and Fort Fronsac was never re-established.

During the next sixty-odd years little happened in the way of establishments in Miramichi. It is believed that there were small pockets of French and perhaps a few Catholic missionaries scattered in the downriver areas. This area appears to have changed hands between the French and English many times.

In 1756, Charles De Boishebert named Beaubears Island the "Camp of Hope" when he arrived and set up a refugee camp on the island. This was built to harbour the fleeing Acadians after the expulsion of 1755 and it is estimated that as many as 3,500 were housed here in a village of 200 houses. Some 800 of these refugees died of starvation or scurvy during the winter of 1756-57. British blockades at the river's mouth cut off food supplies; and much of the food intended for the Acadians and the French soldiers never reached here, but was bartered away to the Indians for furs by the corrupt bureaucrats at Quebec. The dead were buried at Beaubears Point. A monument in memory of these Acadians has been erected by the National Historic Sites and Monuments Board of Canada on the Newcastle side of the river, opposite the island, at Bridgetown.

In 1760, Commander John Byron, grandfather of poet Lord Byron, apparently came to the island on his way from the battle of Quebec and burned the old Acadian settlement to the ground. The Acadians fled to different parts of the province. Some established themselves along the coast, some went to the Saint John River, and a few stayed and settled in Miramichi. From this point on, the island was called Beaubears, a corruption of Boishebert's name.

When the first English-speaking settlers (William Davidson and John Cort) came to Miramichi in 1765, they established a shipyard on Beaubears Island and built New Brunswick's first ship, the 300-ton schooner called the *Miramichi*. Nelson was part of the 100,000-acre grant given by the British government to Davidson and Cort.

One of Nelson's most prominent residents in the early days was John Malcolm, a Scotsman who came to the Miramichi in 1777. He had come with his father-in-law, James Murdock, who had taken a grant in Napan. At Nelson, Malcolm found land that had been cleared by the French. Malcolm's property extended the entire length of the river frontage opposite Beaubears Island. He had married a Scottish Catholic and had converted to Catholicism himself. He was so inspired with his new religion that he built a church in Nelson; the nearest Catholic church otherwise was at Bartibogue, some 15 miles downriver. The construction began in 1796 in the general vicinity of the present Catholic church. His church became known as Malcolm's Chapel. It was blessed in 1811 by a missionary from Quebec and dedicated to St. Patrick because of the numbers of Irish immigrants coming into the area. The St. Patrick's Catholic Church that we know today was built in 1894, from sandstone which was hauled by horse teams across the river ice from French Fort Cove quarry.

By 1790, William Davidson had died and was buried at the Acadian gravesite on Beaubears Point. James Fraser, another Scotsman, and his partner, James Thom, set up a large business on Beaubears Island and here they built a number of fine ships. There was also a huge store on the island. This was one of the most thriving businesses in the province at this time. In 1795, James Fraser was elected to the New Brunswick House of Assembly, representing Northumberland County. John Fraser, James's brother-in-law, took over the Beaubears operation in 1813 and managed it until James died in 1822, when John inherited the business.

In 1832, Robert Cooney wrote the following description of the village of Nelson:

> On the south side of the river, nearly opposite to Newcastle, is the village of Nelson. This is but a small hamlet, containing a Roman Catholic Chapel, two mercantile establishments, a parochial school, and 34 dwelling houses, with a population of 200 souls, chiefly Irish. Abreast to the upper end of this settlement, lies Beaubears Island, on the east end of which, Messrs. James D. Fraser & Company have their establishment. This is the oldest mercantile concern in the country, and was for many, one of the most extensive in the whole province.

The first English name for the Nelson area was Lower Settlement, Southwest. The community was named Nelson in 1805 after Lord Nelson, the famous British admiral who was killed that year in the Battle of Trafalgar. It is believed that the masts for Lord Nelson's flagship were shipped from Beaubears Island. Joseph Russell, a Scottish shipbuilder who bought Beaubears Island in 1837, was said have been a midshipman on Lord Nelson's *Vanguard* in the Battle of the Nile in 1799.

By 1826, Nelson was becoming established. A vessel built at a local shipyard was named *Nelson Village*. Many of the inhabitants were pre-famine Irish who had come in the 1790s or early 1800s. Others came during the famine period in 1847, arriving aboard the *Loostauk*, a sailing ship that arrived in Chatham with many sick aboard.

Another man to play a part in the history of Beaubears Island was Joseph Russell, who had come to Chatham in 1812 and established himself as a master shipbuilder. He had owned the shipyard at Englands Hollow as well as the King's Arms Hotel. Russell sold the Englands Hollow shipyard to Joseph Cunard and purchased the Fraser establishment on Beaubears Island, expanding the shipyard so that five ships could be built at one time.

In 1847, Joseph Russell and his wife, Agnes, built a tomb on the island a short distance from their house. They then removed the bodies of their six children from their various graves and buried them in the tomb. Two years later, their son Thomas died of consumption and was also buried in the island tomb. On February 23, 1849, Joseph Russell advertised Beaubears Island for sale:

Valuable Property for Sale
The subscriber, being about to retire from business offers to sell by public auction, at the court house Newcastle, on Wednesday, the 12th September next, at 12 o'clock noon.

Beaubears Island

With the whole of the establishment for carrying on an extensive mercantile, shipbuilding and fishing business.

The island is a mile and a quarter long, of an irregular width, not exceeding anywhere half a mile. It contains 300 acres of land (more or less) and is situated at the confluence of the north and south west branches of the Miramichi River, near the head of navigation for vessels of the largest class, two miles from Newcastle, the shire town of the county, and six miles from Chatham. There are from 20 to 25 acres of land under cultivation, and the rest of the island is well wooded.

There is an excellent two storey stone dwelling house, pleasantly situated on the south side of the island, near the lower end. It is 40 feet by 38 feet, thoroughly finished, has a frost proof cellar, kitchen, well of water, wood house, coach house, convenient out houses, and a large kitchen garden, the whole being furnished with every comfort and convenience for a large family. The barn will contain from 30 to 40 tons of hay, and stables for five to six horses, besides cattle.

The retail store is situated near the dwelling house, is two stories high with a cellar underneath the whole. The shop is fitted up with the usual conveniences. There is a back store and a comfortable office, with ample room on the upper flats for storage. There is another store, two stories high, used as an iron and provision store, having ample room to contain a large stock.

A wharf runs out into the river in front of the retail store, at which ships of from 5 to 600 tons can discharge and load. On this wharf there is a new store 90 to 18 feet, two stories high, furnished and fitted up as a warehouse.

There is also a salt store, one and a half storey high, close to the wharf, which will contain upwards of three hundred tons. There is a safe and convenient boom capable of holding 7 to 800 tons of timber, between the wharf and the lower end of the island, near which there is ballast berth, which has been used many years. There is also a convenient deal yard adjoining, above the salt store, which will accommodate without any further expense, a million of deal.

The shipyard is also on the south side, about the center of the island, completely sheltered from every wind except the south east. There are now three ships being built in it, each upwards of 500 tons, with accommodations to lay down two more. The yard has attached to it a blacksmith's shop with three fires: a joiner's shop, 40 feet long; a moulding loft of sufficient dimensions for laying down a ship of the largest class; a shed and two saw pits, a steam box and a boiler, and every other convenience.

There is a cook house, with frost proof cellar, well of water, kitchen eating room, bedrooms, and accommodations for 50 workmen.

There is a comfortable house for a foreman, with a barn and garden attached, near the building yard.

The workmen's houses are situated in a range, but distinct from each other, along the south side of the island, just below the yard. There are seven houses, one and a half storey high each: they are framed buildings, finished outside and plastered inside. Two of them contain apartments for three families each; the other five, for two families each. Each dwelling has a distinct appearance, and there is a garden plot set apart for each family. An excellent well of water is situated close to these buildings, and the whole bring in an annual rent of 90 pounds.

There is a good salmon fishery on the north side of the island, and the gaspereaux fishery is prosecuted all around it.

Shipbuilding materials can be procured from the surrounding country, within a moderate distance, and hauled into the yard in any quantity that may be required, during the winter season.

Altogether, the subscriber believes, from his own experience for upwards of ten years that there is not a more desirable or advantageous situation in the lower colonies for shipbuilding; and he is satisfied that any man of prudence and experience might, with the command of a reasonable amount of capital, continue the business from which he is about retiring, with every prospect of making money.

The purchaser of the island may obtain any of the stock and materials remaining on hand, on very moderate terms.

The terms of the sale will be liberal, a part of the purchase money may remain on security, for such period as may be agreed upon.

For further information apply to the subscriber on the premises, to James Adams, Esq., Nelson Street, St. John, or to Mr. George H. Russell, Merchant, Chatham.

Joseph Russell Miramichi, 23rd February, 1849

Beaubears Island was purchased by John Harley and George Burchill, two Irishmen from Cork. They began their shipbuilding in the spring of 1850. These men had worked for Joseph Russell, Harley as a master shipbuilder and Burchill as a bookkeeper and manager. Burchill ran the general store on the island, which was probably the main store in Nelson. He supplied the local people, many of whom were also employees of the firm and had their wages credited against their accounts. Burchill withdrew from the partnership in 1857 and moved off the island to establish himself as a merchant in Nelson itself.

According to Nelson historian Earl English, Harley mortgaged the island to the Commercial Bank in 1866 and, in 1871, the bank sold the island to Peter Mitchell for $2,700. In 1866, John Harley had launched the last vessel to be built on Beaubears Island. In 1879, the entire establishment burned to the ground.

In 1893, Mitchell sold the island to Hubert Sinclair for $2,000. After this the island changed hands many times, coming into the O'Brien family in 1920. When J. Leonard O'Brien died, he gave the island to Parks Canada for a national historic site. The park was opened in 1979.

In 1867, the O'Brien Lumber Company purchased a store in Nelson which had been established in 1830 by Henry Cunard, brother of Chatham shipbuilder Joseph Cunard.

The first post office in Nelson was opened in 1856 under John Kain, who served as postmaster until 1880.

In the 1850s, two Flett brothers, John and William, built a carding mill on the small stream that later became known as Carding Mill Brook. This mill was operated by a water wheel. The Flett boys also had a sawmill on the property.

In 1882, Harvey Flett established a brickyard in Nelson. This was taken over in 1886 by W.S. Loggie Company, who operated it until 1932.

In 1884, a wooden footbridge was constructed across the Miramichi from Upper Nelson (above Beaubears Island) at Batemans Point to Derby Junction. This wooden structure was over 1,600 feet long and was built by John O'Brien of Nelson at the cost of $22,250.00. This bridge collapsed into the river in 1910, just after a woman had crossed it safely.

J.J. Fraser, who was born on Beaubears Island, became lieutenant-governor of New Brunswick in 1893.

At the turn of the century, Nelson was a very industrious community with six mills in operation and eleven general stores. Prominent families in the village were the Sullivans, Burchills, Frasers, Lynchs, Maloneys and O'Briens. All of these people operated mills.

J. Leonard O'Brien was elected MP in 1940 and served in that seat until 1945. He later became lieutenant-governor of the province, serving in this position for seven years.

G. Percival Burchill, grandson of George Burchill, made it to the Canadian Senate.

22
DOUGLASTOWN

The village of Douglastown is seated on the north side of the river connected to Chatham by the Centennial Bridge. Incorporated as a village in 1966, Douglastown has become a modern-day commercial centre, attracting businesses from the established old towns of Newcastle and Chatham. Since the construction of the bridge in 1967, the community has grown in leaps and bounds.

This area was first settled by Scots, shortly after 1800. One of the principal founders of the community was Alexander Rankin who arrived here in 1812 with his partner, James Gilmour. Rankin constructed a fine home in the area and he and his partner soon established a lumbering industry, a sawmill and a shipyard. The Scottish immigrants who followed Rankin to this area named their community Gretna Green. This name was changed in 1825, when Lieutenant-Governor Sir Howard Douglas visited the area shortly after the Miramichi Fire. He had come, as a house guest of Rankin, to assess the damages. The village was named Douglastown in his honour.

Douglastown soon became a lumbering and shipbuilding centre with the chief employer being the Gilmour/Rankin Company. This company had access to a wealth of lumberwoods in which its employees, through an advance-credit system, supplied the firm with timber for the sawmill and shipyard. There were few stores then and the Gilmour/Rankin Company had a general store which supplied goods to its employees. It was said that on pay days the workers were given due bills, which could be spent only at the company store, instead of wages. In colonial times, there was a treasure house of untouched forest at the disposal of the lumber kings.

Like Rankin, other men set up similar operations in different towns along the river. The employees worked long hours, loyal to their company; the owners themselves progressed. It wasn't until the Cunard boys arrived in Chatham, in 1820, that Gilmour and Rankin had any real competition for supremacy.

Great tension developed between these two lumbering companies as they competed against each other for the majority of business. Alex Rankin, who was said to have been a mild-mannered gentleman, represented the north side of the river and Joseph Cunard, the boisterous, self-proclaimed "lumbering lord of Chatham" represented the south side. Both of these men were elected to the Legislative Assembly as representatives for the Miramichi on January 3rd, 1840. In 1843, Cunard was appointed to the Legislative Council, creating a vacancy in the Assembly. When the Assembly was dissolved in 1842, candidates J.A. Street of Newcastle and T. Williston of Chatham ran for the office. Williston won. Street immediately demanded a recount, claiming that some of Williston's men had voted two or three times. A protest was entered. A second election was called in 1843 and it was said that each candidate had a mob at each polling station. Violence erupted at the polls, and rocks, sticks and heavy clubs were in active use for days before and after the election. Someone wrote that it was no longer safe for a Rankin man to be seen on the Cunard side of the river and the same could be said of the other side. Only at midstream could one be neutral. After the election, Mr. Williston wrote a letter *forgiving* all those who would not vote for him "out of fear of being shot" by Street's gang. When a Newcastle bartender named John Ryan was killed in an election quarrel, leaving a widow and small children, the government passed a law that there would be no more elections in Miramichi. After that, for a period, people were appointed to fill government offices, until the "fighting elections" of Miramichi were safely in the past.

It is interesting to note that, during the mid 1820s, a debate took place dealing with the idea of joining the Miramichi towns of Newcastle, Chatham and Douglastown and calling the entire community Miramichi City. This is a debate that continues to this day.

In 1822, the first school in Douglastown (then Gretna Green) was built. This school burned down in 1849 and several fund-raising parties were held to gather money for another school. Dances were held as well as basket socials, concerts and card parties. In 1850, Alex Rankin imported from Scotland an extraordinary library for the people of Douglastown.

In 1830, a marine hospital was constructed on the riverbank near the Rankin home. This sandstone structure was built to handle the many sick sailors while they were in ports on the Miramichi. Appropriately, the stone was imported from the old country as ship ballast. The marine hospital was used extensively as a vaccination centre during the great smallpox epidemic of 1860. The old stone hospital closed in 1921 and today is in use as a Roman Catholic parish hall.

One of the leading social centres of Douglastown in the early 1800s was the Rankin House. This is a huge hip-roofed mansion with twin front parlors facing the river, with a centre hall and winding stairs. The house also held the offices of the Gilmour/Rankin Company.

One of the employees of the company was Richard Hutchison, a Scotsman who had come here with Rankin. Hutchison became bookkeeper for Rankin in 1826 and by 1840 he had advanced to general manager. Hutchison built himself a new home in Douglastown in 1830 and called it the Home-stead. This house stands just down the street from the Rankin House. It was said that this house was furnished in rosewood and mahogany imported from Scotland.

Richard Hutchison became a partner to James Gilmour when Alex Rankin died in 1852. By 1870, Hutchison was sole owner. Hutchison developed Douglastown into a company town by building a number of houses for his employees. The seven houses constructed on Main Street in 1844 were named the "seven sisters" and two larger houses were called the "two brothers." Hutchison had advanced the company in the shipbuilding industry with his "ABC series" of sailing ships, so called because they were named in alphabetical order.

Richard Hutchison sold the company to his son Ernest for the sum of $50,000. The mill burned down in 1884 and was rebuilt in 1885.

In 1890, Ernest Hutchison built a private electric-light plant and the first electricity came to the village. That year, Ernest built his own new home. This house was a fine sandstone English mansion, supposed to have been built for his wife, Eliza-Jane. It was furnished in oak in the 19th-century style. (The house still stands and is now owned and occupied by the Asoyuf family.)

Richard Hutchison died in 1891.

In 1892, Ernest Hutchison gave the Rankin House (then being used as an office building for the company) to the village to be used as an elementary school; it was used as a schoolhouse for more than 90 years. Hutchison also built the Associated Lodge Hall on Main Street, as well as the Miramichi Hospital in Newcastle, in 1915.

In 1907, the International Paper Company of Bangor, Maine, bought Hutchison's mill and named it the Miramichi Lumber Company. This company operated successfully for many years but closed during the 1950s.

Since Douglastown's incorporation, and the construction of the river bridge in 1967, the village has grown rapidly. Its new shopping mall, Northumberland Square, is the largest in the northeast. There are also recently constructed bowling lanes, marina, doughnut shop, car wash and a McDonalds take-out restaurant, as well as the previously established car dealers, race track, aircraft landing strip, museum, schools, churches, lodge halls and seniors' complex. Douglastown also has its own fire department and village hall.

23

THE FIGHTING ELECTION OF 1843

The following is William Wyse's firsthand account of "the fighting election" of 1843, when Alexander Rankin of Douglastown was backing J. Ambrose Street, a Newcastle lawyer, and Joseph Cunard was backing John T. Williston, a Registrar of Deeds, Chatham:

> The polling was held at the Shiretown, Newcastle, one day, at each other parish after that, and the grand total was declared on the last or fourteenth day, again at the Shiretown. This was always the programme at those times in elections, but on this occasion, the Rankin party were not only forewarned but forearmed, as they had piles of stones placed at convenient places, covered with sods or grass, so as not to attract attention, and a cable stretched on stakes, so as to divide the courthouse entrance door, with the intention to have the Rankin voters go in on one side of this dividing rope and the Cunard voters on the other. The Chatham party were late in appearing, and did not arrive till 11 a.m. They took in part of the situation, and the command was given in Irish, to clear away the cable, which was done instantly. They were about two hundred or three hundred strong. The Rankin-Street party, through Big Jim Bass, then got the order to charge, which they did, and the air was immediately full of stones, sticks, and other missles [sic], and a battle royal commenced, but the Chatham party were overpowered at last and fled in different bodies—one through

the woods, coming out that night about Lamont's Mill; another through the woods, but only came out next day at Mill Bank, and the third made directly back to their wharf, followed by the crowd of victorious Street men. They crowded on board the steamer Street George, Capt. Graham. There was a heap of coals lying on the wharf, which the Street party used as missiles, and when she arrived at Chatham there was four inches of coal all over the decks, mute witnesses of the battle.

When the day came for the polling in Chatham, by mutual agreement of both parties the polling was held at Carney's farm, one mile out of town up the river, but for fear of reprisals both parties had reserves ready armed. Cunard's forces were stationed back of Chatham, near the residence of Dr. Pallen (now owned by R.A. Snowball), 1000 strong, and the Rankin forces on the green above Morrison's Mill (now the Miramichi Lumber Company's Rossing Mill) about 500 strong, and mounted men galloped back and forth between the polling place and the reserves of both forces, a sort of signal moving telegraph, bearing news, but the day passed off quietly.

Then the following days, when the polling was up or down the river, steamers or sailing craft were used to convey voters and fighting men to the polls by both parties.

The day of the siege. In some way a rumour was started that the Rankin party intended to ship a gang of fighting men to Chatham in reprisal to avenge some affront or irregularity which had occurred. They were said to intend turning certain voters out of doors with their families and tearing down their houses. This was a few days after the Chatham polling and I think on a Friday. The Chatham folks were not to be caught napping, so everyone was astir bright and early and down on Peabody's Wharf watching for developments, except those that were preparing the barricades. These consisted of two 14-inch squared timbers, one at the corner where the Canada House now stands and the other at the Golden Ball Corner. Three cannon were lashed to these and loaded with scrap iron and spikes, and cart loads of stones were dumped down there to form an obstruction or defence wall and furnish ammunition for the unarmed. These two barricades commanded perfectly the egress from Peabody's Wharf, the only point where the enemy could well land. Peabody's Wharf was crowded with people looking with anxious eyes over to Douglastown. I was among them. The women and children were sent out of town for safety. The morning was beautifully bright and clear, and the red shirts could be seen quite distinctly at Douglastown, embarking in eight or nine vessels. But now, a thunder storm, with lightning of unprecedented severity, set in with floods of rain and the wind veered to the east; but not a man left his post, and after the storm had partially passed, the vessels were seen heading down the river towards Chatham. The first tact [sic] fetched the ballast heaps, a mile above Chatham, the next to where Munro's Mill now stands, and the third, Peabody's Wharf. They came in very close, almost touching the wharf, evidently enjoying the fright they were giving us, and then stood off for Currie's on the other side. They were going down to a polling place down the river, Bay du Vin or somewhere, and perhaps started the rumour themselves for fun.

At last the contest was over and Mr. Street was returned, but enmity between the parties was very bitter for a year or more, so that very few ventured to cross the river into the enemy's camp.

I saw a young man from the Rankin party, who had come over from Douglastown to Chatham, kicked and cuffed from Water Street, to Coulson's Slip, where the ferry boat crossed at that time, and was very badly hurt

A night or two after the election, some one went around after everybody had gone to bed, and marked the windows or doors with tar, of every Rankin voter, or suspected sympathizer, and he was boycotted.

The Rev. Robt. Archibald, minister of St. Andrew's wished to vote for Rankin, who was one of the most liberal patrons of his church, but apparently did not dare to in town, so he went to Derby to record his vote; but that did not make any difference, as the manse was stormed and considerable damage done. It was a little stone cottage that stood where the Miramichi Pulp and Paper Company's Mill now stands, a little back from the street. His congregation was divided in politics and the feeling was so strong that he concluded to resign and return to Scotland. I was present when he preached his farewell sermon, and my sympathies were with the Rankin party, and although young, I often carried their flag in processions and had occasionally to lay it down and fight for it. During the service a lady went out and as she passed up Water Street she saw a party of men approaching, throwing stones down into the river. She rushed back to the door of the church and screamed at the top of her voice, "They are on us." She evidently thought they were going to storm the church. The congregation rushed out, and went to see what was up. They found a party of the rough element of the Chatham party, keeping a jelly [sic] boat load of Rankin men from landing at the church. They called out to the people coming out of the church, "Go back to your service, but these men are not going to land." The feeling was so strong that the government at the next session passed a bill giving Northumberland four members, so that there would be two from each side of the river.

24
THE RANKIN HOUSE

As ancient is this hostelry
As any in the land may be,
Built in the old colonial day
When men lived in a grander way
With ampler hospitality.

- Longfellow

    The Rankin House, Douglastown, was first built by Alexander Rankin in 1812. It burned down and was rebuilt in 1838. It served as a school for over ninety years but has since been restored and is now used as a museum. (Miramichi Historical Society)

The Rankin House is a huge mansion of two and one-half storeys that overlooks the Miramichi River, in the village of Douglastown. A house was first constructed on this site by Hon. Alexander Rankin in 1812.

This spacious wood-framed building, with its hipped roof and massive fireplace chimneys, as it stands today is a kind of monument for this village's most industrious pioneer and politician. Indeed, during the early 1800s the Rankin House was a social centre widely known for its high standards of hospitality to both the white man and the Indian. Today, the house stands as it did in those times, revealing some of the personality of its designer, Alex Rankin.

Rankin was an ambitious young gentleman who came to the Miramichi from Renfrewshire, near Glasgow, Scotland. He was the founder of Gilmour, Rankin and Company, a shipbuilding firm which was an offshoot of Pollock, Gilmour and Company of Glasgow. It was said that Pollock, Gilmour and Company at one time owned the largest fleet in the United Kingdom, and many of their ships were built here in Douglastown. In fact, a great rivalry had developed in the early 1800s between Gilmour/Rankin and the Chatham shipbuilding firm, the Cunards.

The town of Chatham had been established just a few years previously, but Rankin and James Gilmour had set up their headquarters in an area slightly upriver and on the opposite side. Here they cleared the land and erected living quarters and offices. A sawmill was built and the shipyard was established. The elm-shaded back yard sloped away toward the shipyard and open moorlands along the river, while the front garden had a private entrance guarded by huge iron gates. Also on the property was a company store which was located down by the river's edge. An underground tunnel extended from the store and wharf up the hill to the basement of the mansion. (This tunnel was to give safe indoor passage to the wharf and store where spirits were sold.)

The first liquor licence in this village was issued in 1818 to Gilmour and Rankin. The Miramichi had developed a rough and rowdy reputation: it was the height of the rum-drinking era. As one man put it, "If I am to spend another winter on this God-awful forsaken river, I'll need plenty of rum."

By the autumn of 1825, the community around the Rankin House (Gretna Green) consisted of some 75 wooden buildings strung together along a street on the riverbank. At this time the Miramichi River valley was a virgin forest of tall pine trees. These were prized in the shipyards as masts as well as being used in boat construction.

But 1825 saw unusually dry seasons and when the great fire came, on October 7, the saplings exploded into torches, their flames leaping rivers in the path of the forcing winds. Entire villages and towns were wiped out along both sides of the river. The fire swept everything in its path—even the ships in the harbours burned. In just a few hours, one-fifth of the land mass of New Brunswick had burned. One hundred and sixty-five people perished in the flames or were drowned. Nearly three times that number were badly burned or injured and 2,000 were left destitute. Out of the 75 buildings in Douglas-town, only six survived the inferno. One of these was the Rankin House.

The post-fire days saw white men and Indians alike running helter-skelter throughout the communities, seeking relief for their wounded and dying and searching through rubble for belongings. The Rankin House became a refuge for hundreds of homeless people. It served both as a hospital and as a headquarters for the distribution of relief shipments that were sent in from outside. Rankin contributed from his own pocket.

Until now, the village had been called Gretna Green. The lieutenant-governor of the province, Sir Howard Douglas, visited the area shortly after the fire to assess the losses. The village's name was then changed to Douglastown in honour of the visitor.

Two years after the fire, Rankin was elected to New Brunswick's House of Assembly and the mansion became more a social centre, especially around election time. Among the Rankin supporters there were politicians, businessmen, shipmen, millmen and woodsmen who toasted Rankin when he was victorious at the polls. Among these people were many names that are still common in Miramichi: the Hutchisons, Ritchies and Fergusons were relatives of Rankin, and the Falconers, MacLeans, Andersons, Hendersons, Scotts, Lemonts, Alexanders and Hutchisons were employees. Most of these people had come to Miramichi from Scotland with Rankin and Gilmour.

Ten years after the Miramichi Fire, the Rankin House burned to the ground when an oil lamp toppled from a parlor table. All that remained were a smouldering stone foundation and the swinging front gates that squeaked restlessly in the wind.

The Rankin House was rebuilt in 1837 on the foundation. The new house was constructed by William Murray, a well-known builder of that day. It contained 12 fireplaces, including cast-iron ovens in the kitchen. The house also had a slate roof and was framed with timber 14 inches thick. The house became more than just a residence; it housed the offices of Gilmour and Rankin as well as the residence for the clerks, servants and the Rankin family itself.

In 1846, Alexander Rankin was made a member of the Legislative Council of New Brunswick. He remai·ed a member of the House of Assembly until his death over·.as in April of 1852. At this time, Richard Hutchison became a partner to Gilmour and by 1870 he had become full owner of the firm.

When the news of Rankin's death reached the Miramichi, the river folk, who dearly loved a pageant, arranged a funeral procession in his honour. Following an empty coffin, the villagers marched from the Rankin House to St. James Presbyterian Church in Newcastle where an appropriate sermon lauded his uprightness and charity and his support for church and state.

In 1890, the Rankin House was converted into a schoolhouse. The huge iron gates were taken down and later installed at the entrance to the historic gravesite at the Enclosure, Wilsons Point. The Rankin House served the village of Douglastown as an elementary school for 90 years. Recently, the Golf Club constructed a new clubhouse at the back adjacent to the old stone house.

In 1984, as a bicentennial project, the Miramichi Historical Society gained custody of the building. Federal and provincial funding was acquired to start a complete restoration of the house and grounds. The building is now in use as a museum, the headquarters for the Miramichi Historical Society.

The late Dr. Louise Manny recorded in her memoirs, a century after Rankin's death, that an old Indian woman had told her this: "There was once a white man who was kind to the Indians and because of that, when the great fire was sent to destroy the white men that were bad to the Indians, his house was spared. His name was Rankin."

The Rankin House stands once again in its former glory, as if the spirit of Alexander Rankin himself still remains in this Miramichi village. He was indeed one of this river's most admired and respected gentlemen.

25
THE PETERS MANSION

The Peters Mansion, Bushville, was built by Thomas Peters in 1825. It is still in use, as a clubhouse for the Miramichi Golf and Country Club. (*John Burchill*)

The old stone clubhouse at Miramichi's Golf and Country Club, Bushville, is one of the most stately and charming buildings on this river. Once a private home, this stone mansion was constructed in 1825 by Thomas H. Peters, a United Empire Loyalist who was then believed to be the wealthiest man on the Miramichi River.

As a reputable frontier lawyer in the early 1800s, Tom Peters handled most of the region's major lawsuits and land deals, administering his personal advice to many of the settlers of the northeast. In later years, Peters' reputation would lead him to hold such offices as clerk of the court, clerk of the common pleas and surrogate judge of probates and local council, appointed by the Hon. Ambrose Street, then attorney general of New Brunswick and a member of the Legislative Council of the province.

Nowadays, Tom Peters is best remembered for his elegant stone mansion, located on a slope overlooking the Miramichi River, halfway between the twin towns of Newcastle and Chatham, in the countryside known locally as Bushville.

Indeed, Bushville was a perfect location. The mansion was sheltered from the northeastern storms by a tall grove of pine trees and shaded on the south by oak, lime and mulberry trees, while its graceful front garden featured old elm trees that lined a driveway. The white fences encircling the property met at huge front gates.

Nearby, the Bushville Wharf accommodated the riverboat passengers, while the sailing vessels that breezed past to the ports of Newcastle and Nelson added a touch of romance to the setting. The white-pillared Peters mansion was considered one of the most beautiful estates in New Brunswick.

The house itself was said to be a copy of a New York manor, handsome and elegant in every detail. From its formal front entrance, the lavish hallway (with winding stairway) was opposed by a huge dining room and front parlor. The full-length windows in these rooms were shuttered both inside and out and there was a stove alcove in the parlor, with hearths front and rear, the kitchen scullery in the wing at the back, and an extended ranch-style piazza facing the river.

On October 7th, 1825, the house was still under construction, when the great Miramichi Fire swept through the region, burning everything in its path. Fortunately for Peters, his house and the grounds were spared from the flames, which were hampered somewhat by the open farmlands.

Here, in his stone mansion, Judge Tom Peters and his wife (Mary McLean) raised a family of six children: James, Mary, Caroline, Jane, Margaret and Thomas. Mary, the oldest daughter, married Joseph Cunard, the shipbuilder of Chatham. Judge Peters's youngest son, Thomas, died in 1841. Tom

Peters's wife and their daughter Elizabeth died in 1844. The rest of the family married and left the Miramichi and Judge Peters remained in his homestead alone until his death in 1860.

Two years after Tom Peters died, the house and property were purchased by another lawyer, William Wilkinson. In the summer of 1862, when Wilkinson moved into the Peters house, he was a promising young law student, 36 years of age. He brought with him his family and his father-in-law, Rev. Samuel Bacon, son of the famous sculptor, John Bacon.

Wilkinson had arrived in Chatham on September 11, 1840, after a 49-day voyage from Liverpool, England. He enrolled as an attorney in 1847 and was called to the Bar of New Brunswick in 1849. By 1851, Wilkinson had been named surrogate and judge of probates for the County of Northumberland, a post he fulfilled until his resignation in 1870, when he was appointed to examine land titles for the Intercolonial Railway. Two years later, Wilkinson was made emigrant agent for Northumberland by the federal government. By 1881, he was judge of the County Courts of Northumberland, Gloucester and Restigouche. At this time, the east wing at the rear of the mansion held Judge Wilkinson's chambers and law offices.

Wilkinson was said to have been a generous man, offering the house and grounds to churches for their Sunday School picnics.

Judge Wilkinson and his wife, Eliza, were the parents of six children, three of whom died very young. One of the daughters, Eliza, had married John P. Burchill, a local man, son of George Burchill, the prominent Miramichi industrialist.

It was said that Judge William Wilkinson was the oldest member of the legal profession in New Brunswick at the time of his death on November 22, 1918, at the age of 92.

The late Senator G. Percival Burchill, son of John P. Burchill and grandson of Judge Wilkinson, was instrumental in acquiring the old stone mansion and the adjacent farmlands for the development of the Miramichi Golf and Country Club. The golf club was organized in 1925.

Today, the old stone mansion stands unchanged since its construction in 1825. In the mid 1980s, the golf club constructed a new clubhouse adjacent to the old stone house, in the back. The dining room sideboards (imported by Tom Peters) and parlor mantles display mahogany and old silver in the rich elegance of a stone mansion unique in these parts.

Only the grounds have taken on changes through the years. The golf course has been designed and redesigned several times since 1925. Among private clubs, it stands as possibly the most challenging 18-hole lay-out in the northeast. The narrow fairways and small greens protected by pine trees, the sand and the water, all come into play and challenge its players to a true test of golfing skills where each stroke depends upon previous shot placement. And of course the clubhouse remains one of the most attractive in this country.

26
CHATHAM

The town of Chatham is located on the south side of the Miramichi River about five miles downstream from Newcastle. Here the river is five-eighths of a mile wide and up to 46 feet deep at the harbour. Incorporated in 1896, the population varies around 6,700. Chatham is now undergoing modern developments in its port facilities as well as the establishment of government offices and new industries. There is also an increasing summer tourist trade here. The two major highways that lead to Chatham are Route #11 from Moncton and Route #8 from Bathurst and Fredericton. Rail service is to the station in Newcastle.

Chatham has modern subdivisions, shopping malls, schools, restaurants, lounges and a movie theatre. There are several motels here and the waterfront is the proposed location for a major park and recreation area including a marina and amphitheatre. Chatham also has the largest Canadian Armed Forces Base in Eastern Canada as well as a commercial airport which offers regular flights to larger centres. This town can also boast the finest theatre on the river, which is located in James M. Hill High School and is the stopping place for touring Theatre New Brunswick plays.

Chatham is largely an Irish town, having been settled in the early 1800s by an influx of Irish emigrants. This is the home of the annual North American Irish Festival in July. St. Michaels Roman Catholic Church (formerly a cathedral), Mount St. Josephs Extended Care Unit and the Hotel-Dieu Hospital make up the sandstone complex of large buildings on the hilltop. The former St. Thomas University campus buildings in the same area now house the Miramichi Community College.

Chatham is famous for its wealth of stately old homes, many of which are well preserved from the past century. Points of historic interest here are the Miramichi Natural Historic Museum (1909), W.S. Loggie Cultural Centre (including the 1830 Cunard summer house and carriage house, now a children's theatre), Middle Island Provincial Park, St. Michaels Historical Museum and Rectory (home of the town's first hospital), John T. Williston's stone house (Chatham's oldest residence, built in 1824), Beaverbrook Centre (town hall and library), Beaverbrook Arena (gift of Lord Beaverbrook), Englands Hollow Park (once a shipyard), Elm Park (1904), Miramichi Agricultural Exhibition (1903, one of the oldest annual exhibitions in the province), and St. Pauls Anglican Church, Chatham Head (1823, the first church on the Miramichi). The Miramichi Golf and Country Club is located on the highway between St. Pauls Church and the town of Chatham.

Francis Peabody, a trader and a merchant, is considered to be the founder of Chatham. Peabody was born in Massachusetts on November 9, 1760, the son of a Captain Francis Peabody. He grew up in Maugerville, N.B. and involved himself in trading. He worked from his schooner, trading along the coast; one of his stops was in Miramichi where he may have obtained a license to sell liquor as early as 1799. It was said that he would bring with him whatever the people of Miramichi wanted, in return for money or for fish which he would sell in Halifax. In October of 1801, Peabody purchased a lot of land in the area that is now Chatham's Water Street and it was around this property that the town grew. He named the area Chatham after William Pitt, the Earl of Chatham who had died in 1778, of whom he was an admirer.

In Chatham, Peabody became a merchant and a shipbuilder. He had stores located on either side of the road (Water Street). His shipyard was at Englands Hollow further downriver. Peabody was an honest merchant who was highly respected by the river folk for his fair prices. Someone wrote, "He is by far the most extensive and respectable merchant on the banks of the Miramichi." Indeed, Francis Peabody was a well-liked man; so much so that in 1837, when he was an old man, his many friends in Chatham hired Albert G. Holt, a Boston artist, to come to Chatham to paint Peabody's portrait.

It was said of the portrait that "a more striking likeness could not be imagined—the snuff-box, especially, is inimitably portrayed." The portrait was presented to Mr. Peabody, and then hung in the King's Arms Hotel for public viewing before going to the Peabody home on Water Street. Francis Peabody died on July 4, 1841, at the age of eighty-one. He is buried at St. Andrews Cemetery, Chatham.

The sailing ship "Gateneau" as she arrived in Newcastle. This kind of vessel carried the many Irish immigrants of th enineteenth century. (J.C. Miller)

During the early 1800s, many Irish settlers came to the Miramichi. There had been an influx of Scots before this and lumbering had begun to flourish as well as the shipbuilding industry. It was said that anyone could stand on the hilltop in Chatham and count more than 100 sailing ships on the river at any one time. By 1814, the Chatham district had been made into a parish.

After 1815, the Irish emigration increased, the region having gained a reputation in Britain for the high quality of its white pine. Many people got into the lumber business and the merchants thrived. James Fraser wrote, "The youth of the country spent their winter in the woods and their summer lounging about the taverns, a superabundance of which, like weeds, had vegetated under the genial influence of good times."

In 1819, timber prices fell and many merchants failed, some of whom were arrested for bad debts. There was high unemployment. The new Irish emigrants in their idleness began to create a disturbance. According to Fraser, "The local magistrates were all but powerless against such a group. On several occasions arrests were made, but the jail, not being a very strong building, was broken open by friends of the prisoners." A detachment of the 74th Regiment was brought to Miramichi to restore order; with many sailors in port during the summer, the local police alone were unable to control the mobs.

By 1823 the lumber markets had improved, and by 1825 there was a great export of timber from Miramichi. Fraser wrote, "In the fall of 1825, a large fleet carried the following from Miramichi, the skipper averaging no more than four shillings per ton; three hundred fifty one vessels carried 155,040 tons pine timber, 1300 tons hardwood, 3161 cords lathwood, 1,069,260 sup. ft. of deals, 1752 spars, 615 pairs of oars, 1418 hand spikes, 48,683 staves, 38 cords of staves, 103,369 stave billets, 627 sup. ft. birch plank, 228 poles, 220 rickers and 1 mast."

In 1820, pledges were taken toward the construction of an Anglican church for Miramichi. There was disagreement over its location as both Newcastle and Chatham wanted the church. In 1823, the church was built in Bushville, about halfway between the two towns on the Chatham side of the river. It was built by William Murray, a master builder of that day, and named St. Pauls. Bishop Inglis consecrated the church on October 1, 1826. The first priest of St. Pauls was Rev. Samuel Bacon of London. Many influential people of that day attended St. Pauls Church, including the Cunard brothers (shipbuilders, and Chatham's largest employer) and John Mercer Johnson, Chatham's Father of Confederation.

The great fire of 1825 did not affect Chatham directly. It was largely to the rear of the town and the worst destruction was on the opposite side of the river in Douglastown. Chatham, however, involved itself, sheltering the homeless and providing relief to the victims.

The spring of 1826 saw very little run-off in the streams and a generally "poor freshet" made it difficult to get the winter's lumber driven from the woods to the mills. On June 20, 1826, the following article appeared in the *Royal Gazette*: "One hundred and 24 square rigged vessels have already been entered at this port since the opening of the navigation and although much of the timber made last winter is yet lying in the brooks for want of water to drive it, we do not apprehend any scarcity."

James A. Pierce of Halifax established a newspaper, the *Mercury*, in Chatham that year.

The emigrant ships, many from Ireland, continued to sail into Chatham. Most of these ships had illness on board. The *Nicholas* arrived from Belfast in 1826 with ninety passengers. The *Martin* out of Limerick landed forty passengers that summer.

James Fraser wrote, "It appears 1827 was an even more active year. 'The Foveran,' under Captain Moore, was quarantined at St. Andrews Point in May with about two hundred fifty passengers on board. By May 29, the Chatham Mercury reported, 'The number of emigrants who have already arrived at this port is about 1500.' In July the 'Eleanor' arrived with about two hundred aboard and much sickness."

A quarantine station was erected on Middle Island in 1827. This was immediately filled with typhus and dysentery patients. There were also six convalescent patients, for a total of thirty at the station. A public meeting was held to raise funds to build a second building on the island. This building was ready for use on August 7th and was in turn soon filled with the sick. Boat after boat loaded with Irish emigrants continued to arrive in Miramichi.

Sheldrake Island, further downriver off the shores of Loggieville, was purchased and a quarantine station established. The buildings from Middle Island were hauled down the river on the ice and put to use on the more remote Sheldrake Island, where they were filled with lepers. In 1834, a new fever hospital was erected in Chatham.

Adam Dixon Shirreff was granted Middle Island in 1830. He established a mackerel and gaspereau fishery there, as well as a packing industry, and built a house. It was said that several thousand barrels of fish were cured in buildings 120 feet in length by 50 feet wide. It is believed that Shirreff became indebted to Joe Cunard and lost the island to him. He remained bitter with Cunard, carrying the grudge to his deathbed.

In 1847, Joseph Cunard gave the island to be used as a quarantine station, when the *Loostauk*, originally bound for Quebec, changed her course and headed to Miramichi because of the large number of sick and dying on board. The deserted fish-curing sheds of A.D. Shirreff were to house the patients, the Sheldrake Island lazaretto being filled. When the *Loostauk* left Europe she had 467 passengers on board. One hundred and seventeen had died on the crossing and 100 more were seriously ill. When the large packing sheds on the island were filled, tents were pitched on the island's west end. The conditions were bad. One survivor wrote, "Those sheds were as cold as barns, I could see out through the cracks in the walls without any difficulty."

On July 2nd, 1847, the Chatham *Gleaner* recorded:

Dr. John Vondy died while attending the Irish emigrants who had contacted ships fever and were quarantined in some very poor quarters at Middle Island. Last week, we announced the illness of Dr. Vondy, the health officer at the lazaretto: and it is our painful duty to record his death. He fell a sacrifice to that alarming disease, with which of the ill-fated ship 'Loostauk' were visited, and expired on Friday morning of last, about 8 o'clock. His remains were placed in a double coffin, made perfectly air tight and conveyed from Middle Island to Coulson's Slip and from there to St. Pauls Churchyard, followed by an immense concord of people.

We have seldom witnessed an occurance that cast so deep a gloom over the community. As soon as his death was announced, all the shops were closed and business partially suspended throughout the day. The sum of 60 pounds was subscribed in the churchyard for the purpose of erecting a suitable testimonial to commemorate the sad event, and testify the respect for the memory of the deceased. Dr. Vondy was in the 27th year of his age.

Many of the people who died on Middle Island were buried there but the graves have since been neglected and are overgrown with trees. Today, the island (now a provincial park) has a causeway connecting it with the mainland. In 1984, during the Irish Festival, a Celtic cross was erected on the island, in memory of all those who died there.

In 1835, the Cunard steam mill started. This mill contained five gang saws and three circular saws with machinery for hoisting in and cross-cutting the logs, operated by a fifty-horsepower steam engine. The Cunard brothers, Henry and Joseph, were heavily engaged in shipbuilding, lumbering and mercantile businesses. This was a branch of Cunard Shiplines of Halifax, one of the largest shipping operations in the world, with such ships as the *Queen Mary* and the *Queen Elizabeth* luxury liners. Cunards' enterprising success in Chatham was brief, however, and throughout the later part of the 1800s the town's biggest employer was J.B. Snowball.

On March 17, 1839, a new Roman Catholic church was opened in Chatham. The priest was Rev. Michael Egan. The church was named for St. Michael the Archangel, Father Egan's patron saint. This church was replaced in 1909 by the huge stone St. Michaels Cathedral that we know today. Bishop Barry conducted the first service.

J.B. Snowball arrived in Chatham in 1855 from Lunenburg, Nova Scotia, and established sawmills and a shipping business. He is also credited with building the first railroad into Chatham. It is said that at the height of his career Snowball employed some 900 men. Before his death, he was appointed to the Canadian Senate and was serving as lieutenant-governor of New Brunswick.

John Mercer Johnson was a man of considerable influence in Chatham. He was born in Liverpool, England, and came to Chatham as a boy in 1819. Educated at the Chatham Grammar School, he was admitted to the Bar in 1840. Johnson was elected to the New Brunswick Legislature in 1850 and was re-elected a total of five times. In 1864, he attended the Charlottetown and Quebec Conferences and later the conference in London. He became Northumberland's first Member of Parliament in the federal government, Chatham's Father of Confederation.

In 1880, J.B. Snowball installed the first telephone system in Chatham. The Chatham Electric Light Company and the Miramichi Telephone Exchange were incorporated in 1888. The first general hospital was opened in 1869 by the newly arrived order of hospitalers of St. Joseph.

The Bill of Incorporation for Chatham was passed by the House of Assembly on March 20, 1896. The first mayor was Dr. Joseph Benson. Councillors were Peter England, Andrew McIntosh, W.S. Loggie, R.A. Murdock, John Coleman, James Nicol, George Watt and R.B. Bennett. Later, Bennett became Canada's eleventh prime minister, holding the office from 1930 to 1935.

According to James Fraser, "In the fall of 1898 a new time zone was established in Miramichi. The new time was to be thirty minutes ahead of eastern standard time. True time was to be indicated by Mr. Gould's regulating clock. Each day at noon a bell was to be rung so people could adjust their time pieces. The new time was six minutes slower than that previously used by the passenger steamboat 'Nelson.' Much conflict by the various towns, boats and trains agreed on one time and the new time was henceforth avoided."

The Miramichi Agricultural Exhibition Association was incorporated in 1902, and the first exhibition was held in Chatham in the following year.

Lemuel John Tweedie was made premier of New Brunswick on September 1st, 1900, upon the resignation of Premier Emmerson. Tweedie served as premier until his appointment as lieutenant-governor on March 5, 1907. He served in that position until 1912.

The population in Chatham by 1911 was 6,446 and plans were being made for the new Hotel-Dieu Hospital which opened in 1913.

In 1967, a new bridge was erected across the Miramichi connecting Chatham with Douglastown. It was called the Centennial Bridge, to mark the 100th anniversary of Confederation.

Chatham's Frank McKenna was elected premier of New Brunswick in 1987. His Liberals won every seat in the Legislative Assembly, becoming the first government in the history of the province without Official Opposition in the House.

OUR IRISH HEROES

She called, and from a thousand loyal homes
A thousand gallant heroes marched away;
The bearded Russian in his castle domes,
The daring scout that on his blanket lay
Far on the western plains at close of day,
Each heard the summons, knew the stern command
That with deep echoes thundered round the world,
And wondering, paused, to see how hand in hand
Each loyal Britain hailed the flag unfurled.

Our deep-voiced neighbors wished the word for long,
That plunged Old England in this bloody war,—
"Canadians are not loyal" was their song,
And Ireland bleeds from many a cruel scar—
She can't forget the days, though faded far,
When English tyrants spoiled those lovely shores.
And England roused—must to the fight alone.
Vain though, Canadians opened wide their doors,
And to the south her loyal sons have gone.

And Ireland's heart and pride, from every land,
Went forth to battle in the nation's cause—
Beside the gun the first to proudly stand,
The first to die defending Britain's laws.
No marvel at the Boers' untimely pause,
For they who fought, who bled at Waterloo,
Who placed Napoleon on the lonely isle—
Determined they again the same would do
To Kruger: he must die in lone exile.

And this my prophecy—'twill not be long
Ere war clouds lift and white-robed peace return,
With Bobs and Kitchener there to head the throng,

The first to see the fires of victory burn,
The last to strike a fighting foe, I yearn—
With White to counsel, hold, and to advise,
Brave White, who dearly earned a soldier's fame;
Where lives that foe 'neath heaven's azure skies,
That could resist and leave else than a name.

- Jardine

27
J.B. SNOWBALL

Jabez Bunting Snowball of Chatham was one of Miramichi's biggest employers. He was appointed to the Senate and served as Lieutenant-Governor of New Brunswick. (Public Archives of New Brunswick)

In the spring of 1855, Water Street in Chatham was a cluster of false-fronted general stores clapped together like wooden beads on a string. Horse-drawn carriages zig-zagged through the street as shoppers crowded along its plank sidewalks. It was the business district of this bustling Miramichi trading centre.

At a general store called McDougall's, a young clerk busied himself stacking sacks of feed and kegs of flour and tea. He swept particles of grain from the front steps and helped customers load cargo into express wagons. This clerk was in his nineteenth year, white-shirted with broad shoulders. He had a round baby face and a heavy drooped mustache. To store owner John McDougall, this new man showed great potential. He had confidence and he showed a keen interest in the business. His name was Snowball: Jabez Bunting Snowball.

Snowball had arrived in Chatham earlier that same year. A native of Lunenberg, N.S., he had come to the Miramichi to visit his father, the Rev. John Snowball, a Yorkshire Englishman who was minister of St. Luke's Methodist Church here.

Jabez had been educated at public schools in Lunenberg and had attended Mount Allison Wesleyan College in Sackville. It was said that young Snowball possessed a rare eagerness and a wealth of ambition. McDougall, an aging merchant, had become his first business acquaintance in what would be an illustrious career.

McDougall had done a respectable trade at the general store. But now, grey-haired and lame, he depended sometimes on the help of his beautiful daughter, Margaret, who was the same age as Snowball.

Chatham was growing steadily with its shipbuilding and lumbering trades. By now there was an obvious need for lumber mills in the Miramichi region and many small-time sawmill operations were springing up on the rivers. Many of these "jack-knife" operations would not succeed in the rugged northeast. Entrepreneurship was Snowball's strength and he would not merely survive, he would be one of the greatest lumber kings in the province.

Soon after Jabez Snowball had entered the employ of McDougall, the business began to prosper. Together they ventured into lumbering and shipping. By 1857, John McDougall had made Snowball a full partner. This partnership was strengthened when Snowball married McDougall's daughter, Margaret, in 1858.

The McDougall-Snowball marriage was the envy of the townsfolk. Indeed, the young couple was a classic symbol of prosperity and happiness. Jabez constructed a fine new home on the corner of Wellington and King Streets. This was a huge gothic-style mansion with a tower and adjacent wagonsheds. The gardens were always well-tended and the entire property was surrounded by an elegant wrought-iron fence believed to have been imported from England. It was said that the front door of Snowball's Wellington Manor was a one-piece timber, hand-carved by a German artisan. It was here that Jabez and Margaret Snowball entertained their house guests at social functions while commencing the task of raising five children.

But while Snowball continued to succeed in business and to prosper financially during these early years, there were periods of hardship and suffering that resulted in great sorrow for the young Miramichi family. During the diphtheria epidemic in the autumn of 1864, three of their children (Jane, John and Sarah) took ill and died, leaving Jabez and Margaret in bitter grief with two surviving sons, McDougall and William. Margaret, suffering heartbreak and in ill health herself, died in 1871 at the age of 36.

In 1872, Snowball built a large sawmill at Chatham. This mill was steam-operated and at this time was the largest such operation in the province. The firm was incorporated under the name of J.B. Snowball and Company Ltd. The volume of business carried on by Snowball was staggering: as many as eleven sailing ships set in a fleet, awaiting cargo at the Snowball Wharf.

By 1873, other Snowball sawmills had been established in Red Bank and Tracadie. The company also owned a huge farm in the Chatham district that was claimed to have been second to none in the province.

During this time, Jabez had become involved with Maggie Archibald, a Scottish lass who was the daughter of Rev. Robert Archibald. They were married in 1873 and Wellington Manor once more became one of Chatham's centres for social activity.

Jabez and Maggie had five children: Robert, Laura, Francis, Lillian and Annie.

By the 1870s, Snowball was a name associated with employment and industry on the Miramichi. When he was at the height of his career, he also owned several canneries on the Bay of Chaleur. At one time he employed more than 900 men. Snowball cut a distinguished figure with his flowing white beard, stove-pipe hat, cut-away coat and striped trousers. He was a contemporary of the great Nashwaak industrialist Alexander (Boss) Gibson and as an employer he ranked second only to Gibson.

In 1874, Snowball ran for Member of Parliament as a Liberal in the constituency of Northumberland. He was defeated in the general election by the Hon. Peter Mitchell, a man who had been one of Canada's Fathers of Confederation.

In 1878, Snowball ran for MP again. This time he defeated Mitchell. It was said that Snowball had campaigned tirelessly and that it was a hard-earned victory. He sat in Parliament until its dissolution in 1882. He declined to re-offer.

Earlier in the century, Jabez Snowball had become involved in railroading, building a short section of tracks that connected Chatham to the main lines at Passmore, across the river from Newcastle. Snowball was absolute owner of this line. In 1883, Snowball teamed with Alex Gibson to construct more than 100 rugged miles of railway track along the Miramichi and Nashwaak Rivers, connecting Chatham to the city of Fredericton. Sometime later, Gibson bought out Snowball's share of this railroad known as the Canadian Eastern or, locally, the Snowball/Gibson line.

Throughout these years, the Snowball mansion in Chatham became known for the elegance of its hospitality. Politicians, railroad officials, lumbering contractors, ship captains and merchants socialized at garden parties on the manicured lawns of Wellington Manor. Indeed, Snowball's garden parties were the talk of the province.

Snowball had established a Miramichi telephone exchange and the Chatham Electric Light Company, both of which were managed by Jabez's oldest son, McDougall. William, the other surviving son from his first marriage, was assuming more and more responsibilities in the lumber offices of the J.B. Snowball

Company Ltd.

In 1891, Jabez Snowball was called to the Senate of Canada. He held that distinguished office until 1902, when he resigned to accept his appointment as lieutenant-governor for New Brunswick. Snowball retained this position until he died. On February 24, 1907, at the age of 70, the Hon. Jabez Snowball died on the street in Fredericton while walking to a church service at Christ Church Cathedral.

The remains of the late Miramichi industrialist and politician were returned to Chatham. After a state funeral, with a procession through the streets of Chatham, he was laid to rest at Riverside Cemetery on Water Street. This was just a short distance from where he had begun his enterprising career some 50 years before, as an eager young store clerk with a wealth of ambition.

28

THE DAYS OF CUNARD

Joseph Cunard was one of the most colourful and exciting characters in the history of New Brunswick. He was a boisterous man who stood over six feet tall, weighed 200 pounds and was always fashionably dressed in a wide-brimmed hat and a dark waistcoat. He rode—always at a gallop—the largest horse in the country; he had a theatrical zest for life and a love of the spectacular.

Indeed, his vitality and zeal made him a king in New Brunswick's shipbuilding industry. With shipyards in Bathurst, Richibucto and Kouchibouguac, his major operations and head offices were in Chatham on the Miramichi River. By the 1840s Cunard had ventured into lumbering, fishing, brickworks and politics, and during those years (the height of his career) he employed some 1,500 men.

He was a man who was both loved and hated, a controversial figure who was not particularly self-deprecating. His vitality would prove his tragic flaw, but not before his enterprise and short-lived prosperity had led the Miramichi into an economic boom. Joe Cunard was his own worst enemy and his extravagance and slapdash management eventually led to his ruin. He went bankrupt in dramatic fashion in 1848.

Joe Cunard arrived on the Miramichi River in the spring of 1820, bringing with him his brothers, Henry and John. The Cunard boys had all been born and raised in Halifax, the sons of Abraham Cunard, a master builder himself who had worked at the navy yards there. Joe's oldest brother, Samuel, had founded Cunard Shiplines in Halifax and it was because of his planning and his financing that the Cunards came to set up shipyards. He also planned to go into lumbering and fishing under the management of Joseph.

Chatham shipbuilder Joseph Cunard employed 1500 men for a time but went bankrupt in 1848. (*Miramichi Historical Society*)

Soon after the Cunard boys arrived in Miramichi, the ring of hammers and axes could be heard all over Chatham as shipwrights, mechanics, hammermen, caulkers, blacksmiths, riggers and carpenters eagerly set to work at a shipyard called Englands Hollow. These men, five hundred strong, would construct a dozen huge wooden vessels in the first year.

Work halted to the cries of "Shipyard down!" when a vessel was ready for christening. Then the boat was given a name and launched into the Miramichi River. In gratitude to the hardworking crewmen, a shipyard ball was always held on the evening of the christening. These were sponsored by Joe Cunard, and the whole community would go on a spree. Often these celebrations would last for days and the rowdiness that would follow sometimes led to fistfights among the ranks. The crewmen would eventually burn themselves out, take a short rest and then return to work, always loyal to their employer.

Joe Cunard purchased the old Dr. Key house on Water Street and commenced to furnish it to his extravagant taste. There were chandeliers, calf-bound books and mahogany chairs, with a unique harpsichord gracing the corner of the parlor. Near the house there were wagonsheds containing two coaches, stables with a dozen horses, a gatehouse and ornamental gardens. A flock of fan-tailed, bright-feathered peacocks strutted about the grounds. Only Joe Cunard's property could so combine the elegant and the shamelessly flamboyant.

To grace his property, Joe Cunard married attractive Mary Peters, the oldest daughter of Judge Tom Peters from the brownstone mansion up the highway in Bushville. When Joe and Mary Cunard attended St. Paul's Anglican Church in Bushville on a Sunday, it was in a stagecoach (complete with footmen in livery) pulled at a gallop by a team of four black horses. Joe always shouted greetings to everyone along the way.

Joe Cunard was a deep contrast to Henry, his humble and mild-mannered brother. Henry Cunard withdrew from the business in 1841, giving Joseph complete control. Some felt that this was the beginning of the end for Joe Cunard's reign in Chatham, and that the level-headed Henry had contributed a great deal to the firm. He purchased a property up the river at Bushville and established himself there as a country squire. He built a huge mansion (Woodburn) on top of an elm-shaded hill and kept a farm. Henry remained in Bushville on his farm until his death; he never returned to the family business.

Meanwhile, in the town of Chatham, Joe Cunard was making fast deals that were too often staggering in their complexity. He had by now a steam sawmill, a brick-making factory, logging operations and more shipyards. "Joe Cunard is fonder of starting a new business than in taking care of an old one," it was said.

By this time, Joseph Cunard's other brother, John, had returned to Halifax to work for Samuel. This left Joe the only family member responsible for the Cunards in Miramichi. But Joe lacked leadership qualities himself and, when it came to delegating some of the responsibities to hired help, he was indecisive. Many of his staff had no idea what direction they were to follow: a farmer bringing a lamb to sell at Joe Cunard's store could be paid eleven times over, simply by going from clerk to clerk.

In business, Joe Cunard's only rival in Miramichi was a shipbuilder across the river in Douglastown by the name of Alexander Rankin. Rankin was a mild-mannered gentleman who kept a cool business head. He controlled a good deal of the lumber lands up in the far reaches of the river. Joe Cunard was envious of Rankin for this. They were as bitter rivals in politics as they were in the shipbuilding business.

At election time, they were separated not only by the broad river that flowed between their towns, but by their ways of thinking. One was Liberal, the other Conservative. Their respective employees became quarrelsome and the riots that followed temporarily abolished elections in Miramichi. But while Cunard progressed in leaps and bounds for a time, the business of Alex Rankin in Douglastown remained long after Cunard had gone from the river.

By 1839, Joe Cunard had gone to England with his brother Samuel and had gained a contract to carry the Royal Mail. This meant running steamers from Liverpool to Halifax and Boston. The Cunards agreed to build two ships. These were to be iron ships and not the wooden sailing vessels, and many felt that this deal was not that much of an asset to the Cunards. The iron steamship was about to end the age of the sail.

Nevertheless, they celebrated the British contract with great enthusiasm. Upon Joe Cunard's return from England, he stayed overnight in Richibucto, sending a messenger ahead to Chatham with news of the contract and orders to prepare a suitable welcome party for him. This was arranged in a matter of a few short hours and the next day Big Joe Cunard was escorted into Chatham to the sound of a brass band. All of the men on Joe's payroll paraded that day. Huge bonfires were built, fiddles scraped and cannons fired as speech after speech was made praising Joe Cunard as an employer.

Through all this, Joe Cunard had one bitter enemy, and that was Adam D. Shirreff. Mr. Shirreff was a businessman who had run a gaspereau fishery and a packing industry on Middle Island. He had fallen out with Cunard over the ownership of the isand, which he had been granted in 1830. In 1835, Shirreff deeded the island to Henry Cunard, who in turn gave it to his brother in 1838. Shirreff had never wanted the island to fall into the hands of Joe Cunard, and he felt that Big Joe had used Henry to swindle the island from him. Henry Wyse, a friend of Shirreff, said that "the older Shirreff got, the more he hated Joe Cunard." When Wyse went to visit Shirreff on his death-bed he discovered a pair of loaded pistols under the man's pillow.

"They're for Cunard," Shirreff told Wyse, "I'll get him yet." Wyse took the pistols from Shirreff and hid them away in his own home.

By this time the demand for the wooden ship was already starting to decline. Joe Cunard's creditors were demanding payment; his notes were falling due. Many of Cunard's men were finding themselves unemployed, borrowing from Cunard stores.

In 1848, Joe Cunard received a letter from England cancelling his contracts. His credit had at last run out—he was bankrupt.

Speculation about Joe Cunard's bankruptcy was the talk of the town. Rumours spread like wildfire among the many townsfolk who depended on him for a living. Some were already in hock to Joe for food bills and were awaiting back wages. Crowds of men gathered; they formed mobs; Joe Cunard was their villain.

The following is an eye-witness account of the incident, written by Billy Wyse, son of Henry Wyse:

After a short time Cunard came out, booted and spurred on a large horse at full gallop to his office door, where the post office now stands. He lived in what is now the Bowser house. The news of the failure quickly got wind and people in thousands flocked into Water Street, from the office of the mill, labouring under the impression that they were all ruined, as Cunard, they thought, almost owned them. Cunard was closely pressed by the clamorous crowds. He put spurs to his horse and drove him through the crowd. Those who did not get out of the way were run over. Galloping to the mill, then back to the office, paying no regard to those that threatened his life. The crowd threatened to break open the stores and help themselves. Cunard was unarmed at this time. Suddenly, he wheeled and called me, who was standing on a packing case in front of William J. Fraser's store, where Hoffman's is now. He then came over to me and told me to run up to my fathers and tell him to load the pistols and bring them down, which I did, running up the back streets. When I returned, he rode up to me and, as I gave him the pistols, he put one in each boot leg, and returning said: Now, let me see the man that will shoot Cunard. Then he galloped down to the mill and returned, no one molesting. Towards evening the crowd scattered.}

Soon after, Joe Cunard left the Miramichi, riding out in the dark of night. After a short stint in Halifax, he returned to Liverpool. He was knighted in 1859 and died there in 1865. Cunard's obligations and debts were all paid, to the last penny, by 1871.

Nowadays, when Joseph Cunard's name is mentioned in Miramichi, we have visions of a towering man wearing a broad hat, his cloak blowing in the wind; astride a huge white stallion, like a war general, he shouts orders to his men. It was an eager attempt to prosper on a river of broken promises, and a spectacular time long to be remembered as the days of Cunard.

29
THE IRISH INFLUENCE

The Miramichi opened its arms to hundreds of Irish immigrants during the early 1800s, and the Irish influence is strong along the river. Each summer the town of Chatham plays host to North America's only annual Irish Festival. For three days in mid July, Chatham becomes a mecca for the different generations of Irish, from all over Canada and the United States, who come to celebrate their heritage. They number in the tens of thousands.

In many villages along the river the Irish culture is celebrated not only at the Chatham summer festival but also with concerts on St. Patrick's Day. For example, in Blackville, plays are performed at St. Raphael's Hall, while everyone in the community gets into the festival spirit and becomes an Irishman for at least a day. St. Patrick's concerts are also held in other river villages such as Loggieville, Nelson and Renous.

The Blackville production has run consecutively for more than 70 years, its generations of performers showing a religious dedication to both church and culture. The young amateur players now involved are determined to support this festival's longevity. These are local community folk, young and old, personalities who are playing characters of big-city refinement in their own Miramichi hometown fashion. The combination has spelled success and audiences here have enjoyed the theatre, supporting it with a loyalty which has made this the longest consecutively running production in the country.

In Chatham, during the summer festivals, arenas become makeshift Irish pubs; church halls are trimmed with paintings of places in Ireland and used as restaurants, serving corned beef and cabbage or Irish stew; there are parades, with marching bands from all over the continent; there are foot races (the "running of the green"), church services, band concerts, travelogue films and workshops. There are seminars on Irish music, dancing, history, and literature.

The idea of an Irish Festival was conceived in the spring of 1983, when the Irish-Canadian Cultural Association of New Brunswick was formed. Its initial membership of ten people appointed Miramichi's Farrell McCarthy as president. McCarthy and Keven Mann of Bathurst came up with a logo—a half shamrock and a half maple leaf—the "shamrock leaf." The membership also received a lapel pin and an early-Irish poster-map of New Brunswick. "Members especially received the satisfaction of knowing that there was at least one Irish-Canadian Association in Canada that wanted to preserve the Irish culture," wrote McCarthy.

Since 1983, other chapters of the association have been formed in places like Moncton, Saint John, St. Stephen and Fredericton. Each new chapter is duly registered as a member of the provincial association.

"Today we have some 1,000 members," says McCarthy.

But the St. Patrick's concerts, too, have done much to keep the Irish culture alive throughout the many years since the Irish immigrated to Miramichi. These concerts consist of a program of Irish songs, skits, dances and the three-act play. The stage acts are married together by the spirited jigs and hornpipes of a country fiddler. Folks clap their hands and tap their feet, keeping time with the music. And perhaps Betty Washburn, home from England for a holiday, will sing "Harrigan, That's Me." Washburn struts across the Blackville stage with silk tophat and walking cane as she has done since she was a schoolgirl here in the 1950s. For many years Betty's mother, Dorothy, played the piano.

The spirits of past performers remain in the Blackville Hall. Ivan Quinn, with his grey mustache and quick wit, could play almost any role as could Harold Ross, a concert regular for more than 25 years. Tom Ross, a classical violinist, and Dennis Burns, who could play a double role, and a hundred more entertainers seem to return in spirit when the curtain rises.

The late Dr. Monica Donahue, a retired professor from the University of New Brunswick, played a key role through the years, organizing and directing the plays through the 1940s and '50s, the production's glory years.

Old-timers recall the great concerts in those days. They sketch glowing accounts of Father McKinnon, then parish priest, who paced the aisles during a play and toted a shillelagh, putting the fear of man and God into would-be rowdies who threatened the festival atmosphere. A man was once thrown from the hall by the constable at the door for trying to get into the play with a counterfeit ticket he had made himself. On another occasion, a fistfight on the street out front half-emptied the hall; a woodsman in a jealous rage went after one of the actors for kissing his sweetheart on stage.

Father McKinnon would walk from the hall to the railway station (a half mile) during a play to ensure passage home for downriver audiences. Rail schedules were sometimes altered to "play out," the train waiting at the siding until the crowds made it there from the hall. Extra passenger cars were added to both the Express and the Whooper during this week, and people travelled up to fifty miles, lining up at the hall doors hours in advance for a decent seat.

But, since 1983, Chatham's Irish Festival has taken the place of many of the lesser celebrations in Miramichi. The Irish Festival is now a three-day party, celebrating one of this river's most colourful cultures.

In 1984, Sean Gaynor, Ireland's Ambassador to Canada, was in Chatham to dedicate the Celtic Cross, a monument that was erected on Middle Island to honour the many victims of the Irish famine who died at the island's quarantine station in 1847. Many Irish suffered great hardship and death in the course of their immigration here.

Now the festival itself has a new logo and because of it a new term, *Can-Irish*. The logo consists of a tin whistle and the word *harmony*. Harmony is what you get when you come to Canada's Irish Festival on the Miramichi.

30
CLYNE CASSIDY

Chatham's Clyne Cassidy may be the best prize fighter that this river has ever produced. To be sure, his triumphs, both as an amateur middleweight overseas in World War II and after the war as a professional light-heavyweight, leave little doubt of his boxing ability. Cassidy (who was nicknamed Mike or Hop-a-long in boxing circles) was Chatham's sports hero during the tough 1940s, a time in boxing history still talked about for its abundance of great men. Fight fans along the Miramichi still boast that at the height of his career Clyne could knock out an opponent with a single punch. He won the Canadian Army Middleweight Championship overseas and returned home to establish a professional record of 25 wins and two losses as a light-heavyweight, both these losses later redeemed. He became the Maritime light-heavyweight champion in 1947 and laid claim to the Canadian light-heavyweight crown (inviting all challengers for that belt) before his retirement from the ring in 1948.

Certainly Clyne Cassidy came a long way from his humble beginning as a barnyard fighter, growing up on the Miramichi in the hungry '30s. Back then he had worked for the Snowball family on their farm in Chatham.

"It was a lot of hoeing gardens and pitching hay," Cassidy recalls. "Big George O'Donnell was the foreman. He was a rough and tough guy. I was in my mid teens, ten years younger than George. Word got around town that we were boxing and soon a group of lads were coming back to the farm to box in the evenings. We would spar on the thrashing floor of the big barn. We never wore boxing gloves at first. We didn't have any. One evening Big George O'Donnell struck me on the nose and I knew the nose was broken. My straight nose was gone forever.

When I was 18 years old my cousin Billy Murray from New-castle gave me a set of boxing gloves for Christmas. It was more fun after that. But I never took boxing seriously as a sport until I joined the army in 1940."

Clyne Cassidy of Chatham poses, sometime in the 1940s. (Author's Collection)

Cassidy became a member of the 8th Princess Louise Hussars at the age of 21. In training for overseas, he won minor fights on small boxing cards in Fredericton and at Camp Borden, Ontario, before going to Debert, N.S. and then overseas.

In England he was trained by Girouard Van Leeuwan and the great Tommy Farr, the Welshman who fought Joe Louis. Van Leeuwan had been the European heavyweight champion before Max Schmeling beat him for that title. These men taught Cassidy to be a polished boxer instead of a slugger.

"When I first started sparring with these heavyweights, they darn near killed me," recalls Cassidy. "They taught me things about the game—how to pivot, throw combinations, feint a punch and throw a good right hand. I could dance on a skipping rope all day. Later on, I could stay with them. I won the Brigade Championship near Hedley, England, that year."

Like his contemporary, Billy Conn, Clyne Cassidy thought nothing of taking on much larger men. As a middleweight, he sometimes faced heavyweights for the want of a suitable opponent. After the Brigade Championship, his unit went to sea and spent 18 days being "chased to Africa" by German submarines. Clyne fought two fights on the boat and won both. He won two more matches in Africa that year. Later he boxed in Belgium and Holland before going on to win the Canadian Army Middleweight Championship.

"My opponent for that fight was a Canadian Indian from B.C.," Cassidy recalls. "I was weak and tired and had spent a lot of hours in sweatsuits trying to make the weight limit [164 pounds]. I knew I'd have to end it as quickly as possible or I would be beaten. When the opening bell rang, my opponent threw a punch and missed and I countered with a right hand and it was over. It was a one-punch fight. I had a knockout at 13 seconds of the first round. That could be a record."

One month later, Cassidy travelled to Amsterdam and fought a Sgt. Nystram for the light-heavyweight title of the forces. It was a close fight but Nystram won the decision, Cassidy taking a silver medal.

Back in Chatham after the war, Clyne Cassidy turned professional and fought in the light-heavyweight division. He began fighting out of the old Chatham Athletic Association

(CAA) under promoter-managers Vince Moar and "Dode" Daley. Several boxing cards were held which featured Cassidy in the main event. These fights were in the old Opera House, and Moar and Daley brought in fighters from around the Maritimes, Montreal and the United States.

Thousands of loyal Cassidy fans jammed the smoke-filled Opera House to watch their fighter win. They hung from the rafters, sat in the aisles and jammed the ring. Cassidy got $200 a fight.

Clyne recalls the embarrassment of his first fight, against another New Brunswick boxer, in Chatham:

"I had a big reputation then, coming home from overseas with a bunch of trophies and championship belts. In the fall of '46, Vince Moar promoted a boxing card at the old Opera House featuring me in the main event. Thousands jammed into the fight. The local fans and relatives wanted to see me fight. I soon found that my opponent couldn't fight his way through a wet paper bag, nor could he take a punch. Every time I hit that man he went down. I knocked him down five times in the first two rounds. In the corner between rounds, Vince Moar pleaded with me to 'keep the fight going awhile, play around with him, carry him awhile, the fans will think it's fixed if you knock him out too soon.' I went out in the third round, lowered my guard and got hit with an upper cut, which knocked me flat on my back. I hit my head on the board floor and was knocked out. For a time after that, my friends nicknamed me Canvas-Back Cassidy."

Two weeks later, Clyne fought that opponent again and knocked him out. He never lost another fight in Chatham.

Some of the fighters featured on the Cassidy undercards back then were men like Ernie Placide and young Yvon Durelle of Baie-Sainte-Anne. Some of the men beaten by Cassidy in those great boxing matches were such as Billy Landry, a notable Maritime fighter, and Gene "KO" Fowler of Halifax, whom Cassidy defeated for the Maritime Middleweight Championship. After the Fowler fight in 1947, Cassidy went to the States and was featured in places like Portland, Me., Baltimore, Md., and Union City, New Jersey. His training camp was the Jimmy Braddock gym.

But by this time, Cassidy's hands were beginning to give

him trouble; and he found the fight game in the States to be a dirty business, "with a lot of under-the-table stuff" which he wouldn't tolerate. He had enjoyed the fight game as a sport more than as a business. In 1948, he hung up the gloves. Soon after this, he got married and went to work with the New Brunswick Electric Power Commission, a firm he remained with until his retirement in 1979.

After his retirement from the ring in '48, he started a boys' club. Using the old Anglican Church Hall for a gymnasium, he taught young people the value of good conditioning, good sportsmanship and the fundamentals of boxing. Some of the men trained by Cassidy back then were Big Arnold Fleiger, Tudy Moar, Jo-Jo Ahern and the Mally boys. On one occasion, Clyne Cassidy and a friend took a dozen youngsters to Rogersville, where the boys were to box on a card. The van Clyne was driving ran out of gas four miles north of that town and the arena was filled with fight fans waiting for the Miramichi opponents. Clyne and his friends jogged to Rogersville, where they reassured the fans that the fighters would be along later. He and his friend then changed into their trunks and boxed an exhibition bout, while the youngsters were being driven to the arena.

Today, Clyne Cassidy lives in a comfortable bungalow in east Chatham, remaining active in sports and community affairs. As a prize fighter, he never made much money; his largest purse was the $1,250 he earned when he defeated Fowler for the Maritime title. It was the sport he loved most and the excitement that went with it. He modestly relates his many ring victories, reliving each one, round by round, blow by blow. Old opponents fight on in his memory—they struggle on the canvas, listening for the count in the roar of the cheering Cassidy fans.

31
LOGGIEVILLE

A. & R. Loggie Company Mills in Loggieville, sometime between 1907 and 1919. (*Author's Collection*)

Loggieville is the town furthest downriver on the Miramichi proper, where the river is one mile wide. Incorporated as a village in 1966, the population here varies around eight hundred. Loggieville has a community centre with recreational facilities, a fire department, convenience stores, schools and some fine old homes and churches, as well as modern subdivisions. In and around Loggieville there are many beautiful beaches and the summer water temperatures are inviting to swimmers. This is a leisure town, a bedroom community for the larger centres upstream.

This community was originally called Black Brook after the large brook that flows into the river near St. Andrews Point.

Offshore is Sheldrake Island, a thirty-four-acre jagged patch of woodland that looms in the bay.

The first English-speaking settler in Loggieville was John Murdock. He was a native of Scotland who had been established as a merchant on Prince Edward Island but had left the island in the spring of 1777, bringing with him his growing family. John Murdock and his son, George, had received grants of land totalling over 1,000 acres. All of this land was where Loggieville stands today, taking in St. Andrews Point and Sheldrake Island.

By 1783, there was an influx of Loyalists to the area; and by 1791, John Murdock was Overseer of the Poor for the entire Loggieville district. The population on the Miramichi River by this time had grown to 233 people. They were spread out through the downriver areas and this census included Neguac and Bay du Vin. At this time there were two general stores operating at the tiny settlement at the mouth of Black Brook.

In 1825, Black Brook was fortunate to escape the great Miramichi Fire. Many people came to this village for relief, however, and some stayed.

A one-room schoolhouse, built at St. Andrews Point in 1832, accommodated a handful of pupils and served as a meeting hall for the village.

In 1833, the Williston brothers, John and Phineas, built a sawmill on the banks of Black Brook. This mill was water driven, the brook dammed up to form a huge millpond to float the logs. The settlement at Black Brook was beginning to flourish. A one-room schoolhouse, built at St. Andrews Point in 1832, accommodated a handful of pupils and served as a meeting hall for the village.

By 1840, the mill was this settlement's chief employer. In 1849, the mill was sold to Alex Fraser, soon nicknamed Gallopin' Fraser because he was constantly running between the mill and the wharf on horseback to oversee the operation.

By this time, Sheldrake Island had fallen into the hands of James Murdock, who in turn sold it to a justice of the peace. The island was chosen to replace the quarantine station on Chatham's Middle Island, because it was further away from the settled areas. Buildings were hauled down the river on the ice and set up on the island in the bay to house the many people suffering from leprosy, a dreaded disease brought over on the ships. In the spring, when the boats arrived at the river's mouth, the diseased were dropped off on Sheldrake and the healthy continued upriver to Chatham and Newcastle.

It was said that there was a problem keeping the lepers on that island because of the deplorable conditions that existed there. They sometimes would swim across the channel to the mainland. Each time an escape occurred, an all-out manhunt followed until the inmate in question was returned to Sheldrake Island. There was a terrible amount of suffering on Sheldrake Island and a doctor visited there only once a month. The sick received more comfort from the priest, who made regular visits to the island but never got the disease himself. Eventually the lepers burned down the buildings in their frustration. In 1845, more buildings were constructed but the lazaretto was eventually moved to Tracadie.

By 1854, the community of Black Brook could boast a two-gang-saw water-powered sawmill and one trimmer complete, several dwelling houses, barns, outhouses, a blacksmith shop, a small-gauge wooden railway (which ran from the mill to the wharf), a shipyard, a moulding loft, schoolhouse, church, general stores, and a fishery which had been established near Black Brook by the Mackie and Marshall firm.

The old water-powered sawmill on Black Brook burned down in 1855 and in 1856 a new mill was built at St. Andrews Point by Alex Fraser. One year later Fraser went bankrupt, but the mill was purchased soon afterwards by Peter Mitchell of Newcastle. Mitchell was a politician and a merchant who also operated a store in Black Brook. He ran the mill until 1872, the village growing around the mill and the fishery business.

By the winter of 1878, Black Brook had its own post office with the first postmaster being Robert Blake.

In the years that followed, the Loggie brothers, Andrew, Robert and Frank, were the area's best known and most successful entrepreneurs. The Loggie brothers were the sons of Georgina and Alexander Loggie. Because of their success in the business world, Black Brook was named Loggieville in their honour. Andrew Loggie, founder of the A. & R. Loggie Company, was the village's second postmaster and by 1895 the post office acknowledged the name change.

The Loggie boys started out selling such items as pins, needles and slates door-to-door and from this small operation their firm grew into a world-class company, expanding into fisheries of gaspereau, smelts and salmon. They built mills to saw lumber for their own packing cases and barrels and they designed trap nets to increase their catches. They built stores—which were soon rebuilt into larger stores—to handle the growing business, and they opened branches in several towns and villages throughout the northeast. They thrived in the blueberry business. As their company continued to diversify and grow, wharves were built, as well as icehouses, freezers, general stores and schooners. They expanded into Nova Scotia and Maine. In 1914, the A. & R. Loggie Company Limited was registered with $1,000,000 in capital.

The Loggies were responsible for hundreds of jobs and their names were known across Canada and the northeastern United States. It was because of the Loggie business that the railroad line was extended from Chatham to Loggieville. With the railway lines came the telegraph lines. In 1882, Loggieville had telephone communications.

In 1904, the Terminal Hotel was built in Loggieville and for a time, at the turn of the century, the village enjoyed a modest tourism trade due to its railway link to the larger centres.

During the early 1900s, Loggieville had a doctor's office, a drug store, barber shop, ice cream parlor, hotels, dance hall and several churches.

By 1940, all three of the Loggie brothers had died and it was said that they all left sizable fortunes. The Loggies had been plagued by fires, however, and many of the old buildings have gone. Like so many Miramichi River towns, Loggieville has experienced a decline in activity during the past 40 years; but it remains a pleasant residential area with a spirit of community.

32
MATILDA MURDOCK: FIDDLE QUEEN

When Matilda Murdock was just eight years old, her father, David Kelly, went downriver to the Burnt Church Indian Reserve and bought a fiddle from William Dedam for eight dollars. He brought the instrument home to Loggieville hoping that someone in his family would take an interest in it and learn to play some old-time fiddle tunes.

Mr. Kelly could not play an instrument himself but he knew how to tune a fiddle. So he tuned it and left it in the livingroom, where Matilda would pick it up occasionally and start up a *squeak*.

At first she scraped out some old hymns and later songs were followed by waltzes and the easier jigs and reels. Soon she was playing for house parties and dances and was gaining a reputation as the community fiddler.

When she was fourteen, she learned to read music, travelling up to Chatham on the train to take music lessons from Professor Matilda (Maude) Gray. Gray had an orchestra and soon Matilda was playing violin in the group. Matilda combined the fundamentals of fiddle playing with her own style and soon made her first stage appearance, in a play called *The Holy City* which was directed by Sister Marie Harriman of Chatham. By this time she had learned to read music and so she began to write her own tunes.

Matilda still has that original fiddle as a keepsake. Since then she has become known internationally as a fiddle queen. Her old-time fiddle music has been enjoyed from coast to coast across North America. She has recorded two long-playing record albums (with the Ambience recording company of Ottawa) of her own compositions. She has another album to be

Loggieville fiddler Matilda Murdock poses with her fiddle. (*Author's Collection*)

released. She has played several bus tours from Ottawa to Nashville, Tennessee, where she performs at Totsie's Bar; she has won the ladies' category in the North American open fiddle competitions in Shelburne, Ontario; and she's had three guest appearances on CBC's "Don Messer's Jubilee" as well as guest appearances on CHSJ TV's "Earl Mitton Show" and CTV's "Up Home Tonight." She has written over a hundred tunes and has won a few dozen trophies in fiddling competitions around the country.

Matilda Murdock lives in a charming 19th-century house overlooking the broad Miramichi River, on Main Street, Loggieville. The house was purchased by her late husband, Francis, when they were married in 1942. Here, Matilda and Francis raised three sons, Owen, Terry and Leo, and their daughter, Mary Jane. Matilda is now a grandmother and only during vacations does the entire family get together, as Owen and Terry live in Ontario. When the boys come home they all gather around the piano in the livingroom and play music. The family piano is decorated with fiddling trophies, while on the walls are photos of Don Messer, Marg Osborne and Charlie Chamberlain.

"The acceptance of my music by other musicians and music lovers is important," Matilda says. "It's especially nice to hear other musicians playing my tunes."

Indeed, the many tunes that Matilda wrote back in the '50s have been adopted by well-known fiddlers. Ontario's Graham Townsend has used her material on albums and Don Messer played a series of Matilda Murdock tunes on his famous cross-Canada tours.

Today, Matilda Murdock keeps busy. As well as looking after her house and its grounds, she makes appearances with her fiddle at fund-raising concerts and dances. She performs regularly at parties at various senior citizens' clubs around the province. Once in a while, she travels to Arnprior to visit her son Owen and to play at a big barn dance. To be sure, wherever she performs, Matilda Murdock is appropriately recognized as Queen of the Down-East Fiddle.

33
ALEXANDER MacDONALD
HOUSE

Alexander MacDonald arrived on the Miramichi in 1784. He had received a formal education in his native Scotland and was a sensitive man of letters, possessing "an excellent measure of penmanship and an accomplished level of expression." As a youth he had enlisted in the 76th regiment (MacDonald Highlanders) and had served with the British Forces during the American Revolution; his company disbanded in Nova Scotia in 1782. Soon after that, the young soldier made his way north to the Miramichi, a region which had great potential for fishing, lumbering, shipbuilding and farming.

MacDonald was greatly impressed by the abundance of vacant land here that could be had almost for the asking. In Scotland there had been a lease-hold on land and ownership of huge properties was a measure of wealth and prestige. There, only the country squires and the very rich could afford vast amounts of land and a stone mansion. When MacDonald had been on the Miramichi for just a few years he had accumulated 1,400 acres, most of this at Bartibog.

MacDonald built his stone mansion on a point of land where the Bartibog joins the Miramichi, eight miles east of Chatham. In 1815, when this house was completed, it must have appeared magnificent amid the crude log cabins.

The MacDonald house is very similar to Georgian stone houses found in rural Scotland. It is a stately two-storey structure with massive end chimneys and a centre hall. It was once thought that the stone for this house had been brought over from Scotland as ship ballast, but it is a Miramichi sandstone. The slate roof, however, probably was imported from Britain. There were six fireplaces used in heating the house and the kitchen had a huge cooking fireplace equipped with a crane for large pots. The large kitchen featured adjacent maids' quarters; there was a central hall with winding stairs, an elegant front parlor, and a parlor bedroom; and upstairs there were bedrooms on each end, each with a fireplace. The house has many bay windows, front and rear, and each one features the small French window panes. All are equipped inside with decorative folding shutters which are hand-carved. The mouldings on the interior mantles were also carved by hand.

The home of Alexander MacDonald was built about 1815 of Miramichi sandstone. It is an historic site today. (*Public Archives of New Brunswick*)

MacDonald never completely finished the stone mansion in his lifetime. The upstairs bedrooms were left unfinished: perhaps he had run out of funds, or his dream had exceeded his grasp. He had married Grace McLean in 1790 and they raised a family of thirteen. MacDonald farmed the fields around the stone house. He had a huge barn and owned some livestock.

The salmon fishing was excellent in the Miramichi River off the tip of Bartibog Island, and he had the labour of his boys to help him.

Perhaps because of his education, in 1809 MacDonald was given the command of a company of the 1st Battalion of the Northumberland County Militia. He was soon promoted to the rank of major.

MacDonald was also becoming active in various offices in public life. He was town clerk, a member of the grand jury, commissioner, surveyor, overseer of roads, overseer of the poor, assessor, school trustee, harbour master and a trusted advisor to all who sought his assistance.

But MacDonald's life was punctuated by many incidents of extreme hardship and disaster that would have discouraged a man of lesser will. An infant, Gracey, died in 1812. Mary, the eldest daughter, died in 1817 at the age of 23. In 1823, shortly before his eighth birthday, the youngest child, Colin, was killed when the east chimney of the house was struck by lightning and destroyed.

MacDonald himself suffered poor health and financial setbacks during the 1820s. In 1823 a severe accident left him partially disabled. He then sold the house and farm to his son, Ronald, for [L]300.

On December 11th, 1834, Alexander MacDonald died at the age of 72. His wife, Grace, followed less than a month later after suffering a long illness.

The stone mansion stayed in the family until the farm's sale in 1853. Since 1853, owners of the property have included Robert Brown, George Smith and Michael McCarthy.

In the early 1970s, the government purchased the property from Michael McCarthy's son, Allard, and restored the barns, wharf, boathouse and stone mansion. Today, the Alexander MacDonald farm in Bartibog is one of New Brunswick's finest historic sites.

34
THE SNOWBALL/GIBSON
RAILROAD

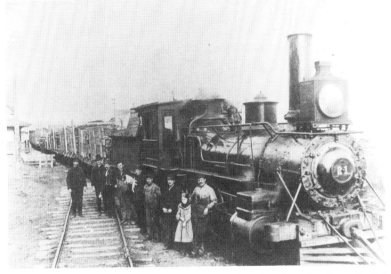

Engine #21 sits at the Blackville Station shortly after the Snowball/Gibson Railway was built in 1886. (*Warren McKinley*)

A brilliantly polished locomotive, Engine No. 21, took on water at the Blackville railway station. Hissing, its wood-fired boilers sent rings of smoke curling over the Miramichi logging town. A nearby windmill pounded and rattled in its gate while it charged a generator. The ringing peals of a smith's hammer on the anvil echoed the clatter of hoofbeats in the street.

Energy was virtually free here, but that was 100 years ago: the region belonged to lumber kings such as Jabez B. Snowball and Alexander Gibson. These two men built the first railroad that ran from Chatham to Fredericton. It was completed in 1886 and was known as the Canadian Eastern Railway or, more commonly, the Snowball/Gibson line.

Snowball, a native of Lunenburg, N.S., had graduated from Mount Allison Wesleyan College in Sackville and had moved to Chatham, establishing sawmills in Bay du Vin, Red Bank, Millerton and Tracadie, with his largest operation in Chatham—a huge steam mill which was then the largest in the province. It was said that Snowball was employing more than 900 men.

Alexander Gibson was a Nashwaak River industrialist. He had several lumber mills, one of which was located in Blackville on the Miramichi. On the Nashwaak he had built a company town: a cotton mill, a brickyard, churches, schools and low-rent housing for his employees. He was known, too, for his great interest in railroading.

Before 1885, the only rail service along the Miramichi River was the short section of tracks that ran from Newcastle up the north side of the river to Indiantown (Quarryville). A branch of the old Intercolonial Railway, it served to haul freight from the quarries in Quarryville and the many mills of the Millerton area. A short "mixed" train also carried a few passengers.

Prior to the construction of the Snowball/Gibson line, Boss Gibson had ventured into railroading on his own. He had constructed tracks from his town (Gibson) to Edmundston, with a branch line to Presque Isle, Me., which was opened in 1881. It was a narrow-gauge railroad and standard-gauge cars could not be transferred from other tracks: this was a great lesson in railroading for Gibson.

Snowball, who was by then a Member of Parliament for Northumberland, had started to build from Chatham to a small junction on the south side of the river (Passmore) where he could join the Moncton/Campbellton tracks.

It was with Alex Gibson, however, that Snowball became involved in railroading in earnest. The two industrialists joined forces to construct over 100 miles of railway tracks through a rugged wilderness, following the Miramichi and Nashwaak Rivers from Chatham to Fredericton. Sometime later, Gibson bought out Snowball's share of the railway and, with Senator Thomas Temple, formed the Fredericton Bridge Company. He then erected the first railway bridge to span the Saint John River, connecting Gibson to Fredericton.

Some claimed that the British government had guaranteed the money for the Snowball/Gibson Railway and had taken part in discussions about the route, which apparently could have gone to the Saint John River valley. A railway through the North Shore of New Brunswick was the route supported by two other politicians of the Miramichi, Peter Mitchell and John Mercer Johnson, both Fathers of Confederation. It was said that the British government had settled the dispute at the Colonial Office in London.

Mitchell, Johnson and Snowball were given the credit by the Miramichi people for bringing the railway here. Someone wrote a folksong which became popular for a while:

Hail storm, Black Tom,
Ain't goin' to rain no more.
The railroad runs on the northern side,
Ain't goin' to rain no more.
Snowball and Gibson will pay for a ride,
Ain't goin' to rain no more.
Mitchell and Johnson will jump on behind,
Ain't goin' to rain no more.

The Snowball/Gibson Railway ran along the south side of the Miramichi River from Chatham through Chelmsford and on upriver to Blackville. There, a huge wooden trestle spanned the Miramichi River. The tracks then followed the north side, winding along the river bends through Doaktown (where it crossed the river again) and Boiestown; there it left the river and followed closely the old portage route through the woods to the Nashwaak valley.

Its construction was undertaken by the Northern and Western Railway Company of New Brunswick. The work crews commenced construction on both ends of the line with a plan to meet eventually in the river's central village of Doaktown. The tracks were opened for traffic on January 1st, 1887.

It was a fully equipped railway line, recalled one old-timer. The smallest communities along the line had plank platform sidings with coal-heated shanties, while the larger villages supported station houses staffed with agents, trolley men, section crews and the occasional extra gang for major maintenance.

The wooden trestle spanning the Miramichi at Blackville was eventually torn down and the tracks moved to the north side of the river. (*Blackville Historical Society*)

Of course, a new railroad through the rugged New Brunswick wilderness had its setbacks and maintenance was required. Some of the long up-hill grades through the Gray Rapids region were almost insurmountable by the woodburning engines of the 1880s. A freight train leaving Chatham with a heavy cargo was forced to a crawling pace as it faced the steepest grades, bellowing black smoke from the engine's burner. (One of these engines would have been No. 21 with its crew of Sye Lawson, fireman, Nanford Rideout, engineer, and Fred Ogilvy, brakeman.) So slow was the train on difficult grades that a hobo could jump on and off almost at will. A boy selling berries by the tracks could climb aboard the moving train, sell to the passengers, and jump off unharmed a short distance from where he started.

But the major problem encountered with this railroad was said to be the wooden trestle that spanned the river at Blackville. This was jarred by heavy ice floes and soon showed signs of weakening from rot. The wooden spans shook under the trains' weight. It was feared that the trestle would collapse, dropping a whole train and its passengers into the frothing river below. After careful examination, the trestle was condemned and for a time the train from Chatham went only that far, unloaded its passengers, and backed up to Chatham again. The same was done on the opposite side of the river, coming from Fredericton, and the passengers walked from train to train.

Records show that a man travelling from Chelmsford to Fredericton on the Express could travel for $3.00 first class or $2.05 second class.

In 1904, the Intercolonial Railway (ICR) purchased the Canada Eastern (Snowball/Gibson) Railroad and the old Newcastle/Quarryville line was extended up the north side to Blackville, eliminating the wooden trestle and joining the tracks on the north side. In 1913, the rails on the south side were taken up. The ICR later became the Canadian National Railway and the passenger arm became VIA Rail.

In the heydays of the railroad, this set of tracks could boast two passenger trains daily, running to and from Fredericton, with a number of freight trains in between. One of these trains was the legendary Whooper, an evening passenger train with an elegant steam engine, puffing black smoke and sounding a forlorn whistle that was almost haunting. The train was named after the Miramichi's best known ghost story, "The Dungarvon Whooper."

The Whooper also carried the mail and, at its many siding stops along the river, woodsmen, farmers, rivermen and their wives gathered to await her arrival. At the more remote sidings, the train just slowed down, stopping only if it was flagged by a passenger. On one occasion the train was flagged at a siding in Lower Derby by a lumberman filled with rum, on his way home from skidding logs. "Skid me off on Howards

Siding," he said to the conductor. The rowdy woodsman was skidded off by the stern conductor just two miles up the tracks, in Millerton. Indeed, the conductors on these trains were responsible for keeping order. Sometimes tempers flared, as boisterous crowds partied their way home from a shopping trip to Newcastle. Among these conductors were men like Jim O'Hern, Danny Mountain and George Underwood.

Underwood recalled an incident where a "high-toned" old stick of a lady, her grip in hand, was getting on the Whooper's rear passenger car in Newcastle. Demanding the conductor's attention, she shouted: "Where'll I go sir? Where'll I go?" Said Underwood, "Go wherever in Christ you like, madam, but don't go upstairs!"

This railway system stood as a kind of symbol, connecting the small outpost communities to the larger centres. It remained in use for some 100 years. Through the 1960s and '70s, however, the traffic on the line diminished to virtually nothing and its trains vanished in a cloud of energy costs. For years, the old Snowball/Gibson Railroad lay idle, a ribbon of rusty steel hidden beneath dead grass.

In the spring of 1985, construction crews commenced the demolition of the line. The last spike was drawn before that year ended.

Today, there is little evidence of the railroad. The line is a clearing channelled through the woods, with only the occasional trestle remaining intact. The shim-shack skeletons along its grades remain as haunts for the hobos who once travelled the line for free. The railroad has now all but faded in a wilderness of growth. The sleek locomotive lingers most clearly in memory, a giant iron horse gleaming in the sunlight of old photographs.

35
THE MIRAMICHI FIRE

When the fire king called forth his legions
    And speeded them forth on the blast,
Six thousand square miles of our province,
    Lay desolate all as he passed.
Some hundreds of persons had perished,
    Some millions of dollars were gone,
And wild was the sad scene of sorrow
    The sun of the morrow looked on.
The fish were found dead in the rivers,
    The vessels were burned at the stocks,
And the forest consumed by the fire
    Till the soil was rent clear from the rocks.
From the hearts of the stricken survivors
    Went up a wild anthem of woe,
While the face of the fire-swept landscape
    Was white with a mantle of snow!
                    - Michael Whelan

Since the arrival of the white man, the Miramichi River had become known for its tall white pines. Much of this region had not seen the axe by 1800 but already it was famous in Europe for its spectacular virgin forest.

This forest was of extreme importance to the early settlers on the river. Their homes were constructed at first from logs and later from hewn and sawn lumber. The lumber industry began to flourish in the early 1800s, as did the shipbuilding industry. England had reserved the choice pines for masts for the Royal Navy. These were exported in Miramichi-built ships. Lord Nelson, the famous British admiral killed in 1805 in the Battle of Trafalgar, had gotten the masts for his flagship at Beaubears, an island at Nelson-Miramichi. While the river's salmon were a valued resource in colonial times, lumber was the river's single most important commodity.

The summer and early autumn of 1825 had been dry and hot. It was one of the dryest seasons that anyone could recall. Robert Cooney wrote: "The summer of '25 was unusually warm in both hemispheres, particularly in America, where its affects [sic] were fatally visible in the prevalence of epidemical disorders. During July and August, extensive fires raged in different parts of Nova Scotia." Cooney described the Miramichi as a large river that was thickly settled for about 100 miles on both sides. There were several towns and settlements, all of which were built of wooden houses, stores, stables and barns. Many of these barns were filled with crops in October, and the warehouses and stores were stocked with spirits, powder and the necessary supplies for the coming winter. The cleared fields and the settled parts of the river formed just a narrow strip "about a quarter of a mile wide. This lay between the river and an almost interminable forest."

On the afternoon of Friday, October 7, 1825, the fire came. Foreshadowed by great clouds of smoke and drifting cinders, it laid to ashes six thousand square miles of Miramichi timberland. In a span of ten hours, one-fifth of the entire province was destroyed. It was said that the fire burned at a speed of one mile per minute and had a twenty-mile front. It had jumped the river in three different places.

Cooney wrote:

> The tremendous bellowing became more and more terrific. The earth seemed to stagger as if it had reeled from its ancient foundations. The harmony of creation appeared to have been deranged: and about to revert into original chaos. Earth, air, sea and sky: all visible creation seemed to conspire against man: and to totter under the weight of some dreadful commission they were charged to execute. The river, tortured into violence by the hurricane, foamed with rage and flung its boiling spray upon the land. The thunder pealed along the vault of heaven; the lightning rent the firmament in pieces. For a moment and all was still, a deep and awful

silence reigned over everything. Suddenly a length-ened and sudden roar came booming through the forest and driving a thousand massive and devouring flames before it. Then Newcastle and Douglastown and the whole northern side of the river, extending from Bartibog to the Nashwaak, a distance of more than 100 miles in length, became enveloped in a [sic] immense sheet of flame, that spread over nearly 6,000 square miles.

The sapling pine trees along the small clearings of the river only served as added fuel and the flames in the treetops were fanned by a downriver breeze and the thunderous combustion of the fire itself. So strong was the wind from the fire itself that it picked up an empty pork barrel from someone's yard and carried it to a neighbour's dooryard on the opposite side of the river.

Ships in the local ports caught fire and burned to the water level. Those still under construction in shipyards were de-stroyed. Complete towns were wiped out; nothing was visible but embers, ashes and smoke. It was said that people dropped what they were doing and ran to the river, wading out in the now warm water with their babies crying in their arms.

Looking back, in 1932, Cooney wrote:

I shall say nothing of the human bodies, some with their bowels protruding, others with their flesh all consumed and the blackened skeletons smoking. Of the headless trunks and severed extremities; of some bodies burned to cinders; others reduced to ashes; of many bloated and swollen by suffocation; and several lying in the last distorted position of convulsing tor-ture....

Newcastle, yesterday a flourishing town of nearly one thousand inhabitants, Douglastown with three hundred, Moorfield, an old and populous settlement and many other heaps of ruins. Trees were charred, crisped, leafless—some standing with gaunt and shriv-elled limbs, many flat on the ground. Thousands of wild beasts dead and dying, as well as domestic animals; myriads of fish—salmon, trout, bass—dead, floundering, gasping, on scorched shores and beaches; wild fowl also and human bodies. Desperate groups of half famished, half naked, houseless creatures, all more or less injured, many lamenting the loss of children, relatives, friends—all deploring the loss of property.

Out of the entire town of Newcastle, only six houses remained. Only one or two houses remained in Douglastown, one of which was the huge house of lumber king Alexander Rankin. During this disaster, Rankin had turned his home into an emergency aid station and hospital.

Word of the disaster spread quickly and contributions of supplies and money were received from Saint John, St. Andrews, Richibucto, Shediac, Bathurst, Halifax, Lunenburg, Pictou, Antigonish, Yarmouth, Amherst, Newfoundland, Prince Edward Island, central Canada, the United States and Great Britain.

Before it finished, the fire ran down the north side of the river as far as Burnt Church. On the south side it swept everything as far as Northumberland Strait. It is difficult to assess the number of dead. Some reports say 150 perished; others estimate the toll at over 250. Twice that number were badly burned or injured and it is said that two thousand were left homeless. Folks covered the remaining foundations of their homes and spent the winter there, underground. Some people moved in with relatives or friends who were more fortunate and others left the river completely, never to return.

The calamity was looked upon by some as a kind of punishment for the wickedness, rum-drinking and gambling that had dominated the Miramichi.

36

ON PAST FAVOURS

(A Short Story)

The community was one of scattered wilderness farms all of which bordered along the river. Each one was apart from the other and had its own personality, the spirit of its owner. These farms were held in a community largely through bonds of respect for the other man's property and his welfare. In a transaction with a neighbour, the nod of a head was as good as a signature. The adults of the community rarely visited. Philosophies were exchanged over line fences at haying time. Imaginations were nourished by loneliness and each one's strongest characteristics were developed from exposure to themselves alone. Indeed, there were characters here in Moores Siding (Miramichi); as a youngster, I knew them all.

There was old Tim Wills, who walked at night talking to himself in a variety of tones and answering himself in imaginative voices so that if you didn't know him and you heard him coming in the dark, you'd swear it was a crowd of men.

And there was old Charlie Eighton from the next farm. Chuck was a confirmed salmon poacher. Folks said that it wasn't so much that Old Man Eighton wanted the fish he caught, but that he got his kicks from the risk of being caught sweeping a pool. For excitement, he would poach in broad daylight. It was in his blood.

The fish wardens in those days were Ed Black and Raymond Mills. Old Ed was obsessed with his career. "I'm sworn to protect the Atlantic salmon," he would say. "A dangerous species." He would help keep the balance of nature by saving the salmon link in life's chain and thus save mankind from extinction. It was said that Ed and Raymond would chase a poacher through the gates of hell. Indeed, all of us at Moores Siding respected the wardens.

In the mid '50s, the fish wardens travelled the river by canoe and they became accustomed to long river runs of two or three days at a time; not an easy life. It was common to see them pitch a tent on the riverbank near our farm and there spend the night. I can recall watching from the hill top and catching the fragrance of fish fillets sizzling on their campfire which snapped by the lee side of a canoe propped among the bushes. While Ray and Ed were from some thirty miles up the river, they soon became close friends of my father as they sometimes used our interval for a tenting area.

One autumn evening, after the salmon angling season was closed for the year, the wardens made camp on the flats as they always did—only this night, Father invited the two men to our farmhouse to share the evening meal with the family. Ed and Ray were treated with heels of rum and the last drop of scotch whiskey in twenty miles. Voices loudened as they talked and laughed with Father, all cronies now in the old dining room.

Ed was telling Father of having given chase to an awkward poacher that same afternoon.

"Yes" said Ed. "He was drifting with a long net, right through the salmon hole, just up around the bend from here and in daytime, the gall of it."

He went on to tell Father of the man scrambling to get away, running up the steep riverbank with the wet salmon net dragging in the grass, a couple of large salmon entangled.

"He ran into a poplar tree top, left there by beaver," Ed continued. "His net caught up in the branches and he had to leave it with a large salmon meshed, dead. But the son of a whore got away, with one or maybe two large salmon."

He then told us the poacher threw rocks from the top hill, trying to hit them while they were untangling the net from the tree branches and putting it into their canoe.

Then Ed proceeded to lecture all of us on the dreadful condition of the resource, the amount of poaching that was going on and the trash that hung around the river in these parts, and how poaching would affect us all someday.

Then a rap came on the kitchen door and without waiting for an answer Charlie Eighton entered the house. Charlie was in a fresh change of clothes, his new plaid mackinaw and his best felt dress hat. Under his arm he was carrying a large salmon of about twenty pounds. He was probably repaying Father for a past favour, or maybe it was just a gift to a loyal neighbour. In any case, the salmon was completely wrapped in newspapers from its head to beyond its tail. Charlie walked up to the dining room table where the men were grouped, the fish tucked neatly under his arm.

When he saw the two uniformed wardens sitting at the table, he said, "Here Jack, here's the rifle I borrowed from you last week."

He passed the long salmon nervously across the table to Father.

"Indeed," said Father and at once took the newspaper-wrapped fish across the dining room and stood it in the corner. He then came back to the table and went on with his evening meal.

When Charlie was gone, the warden was quick to remark, "Now that's my cut of a man."

37

IN KEEPING OUR BEST TRADITIONS

(A Short Story)

It was a four-hour hike through heavy bush from our farmhouse to the old beaver dam on Morse Brook. Grandfather and I had left the house at daybreak and travelled together until we reached the road forks at Sandy Hill, two miles back. There we split up. He had chosen to hunt the north side and I would meet him at Leaning Pine, our traditional lunching place. We'd have lunch at mid-day, visit the barrens and return home at dark.

For many seasons my grandfather and I had spent at least one day here in the brook area hunting deer. As I made my way down the slope in the direction of the brook and followed the valley, I could feel a tingle of excitement and storm-fear that sometimes advances a season's first snowfall.

Sure enough, by late morning the sky had turned grey and overcast as a northeast wind gusting above the tree tops suggested snow, possibly by mid-day. While the dry leaves beneath the alders swirled restlessly about, beyond the flat the poplar ridge stood leafless and naked awaiting the storm. For generations our family has owned these woods and the brook area has served as traditional hunting grounds. There are many landmarks here that can inspire thrilling tales—tales that have been told and retold by kinsfolk whose glowing accounts of hunting triumphs have become family legends. The area has also supplied the family farm with wood for fuel and logs for the one -time sawmill. It is the home of many beaver—and prized bucks.

The newly-inducted coyote has become a worry to us now as a threat to the deer. Coyote packs have been spotted beyond the country line on the higher ridges near the headwaters of the brook.

On that day the brook was still free of ice and it brawled over gravel bars and boulders and made sharp bends where the water ran deep and fast. Then it flattened out into a broad stillwater fringed with meadow grass. A sodded mound below indicated an old beaver lodge and there was a wake in the pond from something that moved below the surface, a beaver or a spawning salmon. On the far side was a mud bar containing deep frozen hoof prints from the deer and moose that had been drinking there. I poked my way through the alders and across the now leaky dam and left the flats for higher country.

The hardwood ridge lay ahead, many acres of black birch and maple with the occasional clump of hazel bush fertilized by a rattling cushion of dry leaves.

A ruffed grouse flew among the leaves before me, although I could hear more than see it. I had no shot, but the quick flight had my heart pounding. There wasn't time to follow it, so I continued across the ridge and into the clean bottom pine country. Here the jack pines stood thick and tall in a brown forest. Big timber I always find awe-inspiring. For a while I walked in slow circles, gazing up at the snow flakes that drifted down among the trees that swayed to and fro like bare masts upon a windy sea.

And then I heard it!

The deer had caught me off guard in my little spell. It thumped the frozen ground not 30 yards away behind some undergrowth. A more experienced hunter would not have allowed himself to be surprised by it. With great ease, the big deer zig-zagged beneath the limbs, waving its broad tail like a banner; it cantered over brush and fallen logs, almost in slow motion, vanishing in the heavy bush near the brook, on its way to the next county. I was left staring in a helpless daze without so much as raising a hand.

Approaching the Leaning Pine area, I found Grandfather moodily cooking lunch over a blazing fire. A blue haze drifted among the tall trees and the autumn air was filled with the aroma of brush tea brewing. He was a man of about seventy then, red-shirted, with iron-grey hair, and stooped slightly from his many years as a lumberman. The outdoors had been his life and he cooked with ease. After passing me a drink of brandy for the chill and piling our campfire high, he talked of his youth, spinning yarns of hunting friends who had gotten big game here. We stood with our backs to the wind as the pelting snow now came in serious fashion.

In accordance with our best traditions, Grandfather served a meal more tasty than any I've had in town.

Sippin' from the boilin' pail, he recalled shooting two bucks "where the horseshoe is hangin'" near the brook's upper landing. They were identical in size, shot on the same day. He remembered shooting a caribou in the barren while still under-age for a big game license. He once shot a big bull moose that came out to the potato field where he was digging potatoes. He said he once came upon two deer with horns locked from fighting. One of them was still alive, but it had to be destroyed.

I would have been content to remain by the fire the whole afternoon, but we still had miles to go and so we moved out in the direction of the barren, our campfire sputtering in the distance.

Shortly we approached the edge of the barren, a vast yellow sea of waving grass and wild cranberry bush stretching silently to the horizon. The stunted red spruce and scattered aspen ringed the edge and the occasional grey rampike emerged from the soggy earth.

"There are no deer here today," said Grandfather. "They're all lying down in 'var' thickets away from the storm."

I thought of our own comfortable den where a cheerful fire and reading lamp awaited us, and I shivered, chilled to the bone. By late afternoon we had satisfied our curiosity in the barren area with its bleakness and chill and at length headed in the direction of Sandy Hill Road and home.

Upon travelling a distance of no more than three city blocks, Grandfather put up his hand, signalling me to stop. I halted in mid-step. He stood peering into the storm.

Suddenly he raised his firearm and discharged its blazing muzzle twice into the darkening woods. The smell of powder and gun oil was heavy in the dampness as the gun barked short in the driving snow like the one-two punches of a skilled boxer. I still saw nothing.

Hurrying to the grove, we found a five-point buck lying motionless beneath the bush. The old man's careful shots had broken the animal's neck.

Its frozen stare was fixed and lifeless, like that of a stuffed game head that hangs from a parlor mantle. There were blood stains on the new snow and right away I noticed the many different sizes of deer tracks here in the heavy woods.

I became eager to check the trampled grove for another deer. I asked Grandfather for approval to hunt a while longer. At length he nodded his consent, but with reluctance it seemed.

"Take 10 minutes, no more," he said. "The folks at home will worry if we're not back soon."

While still in shouting distance of Grandfather, I caught in a glance what looked like a deer beneath some low-limbed trees. After straining my eyes for a better look in the dismal stormy evening, I satisfied myself that it was in fact a large doe, with a smaller deer nearby—possibly a spring fawn. Motionless they stood, staring at me in the snow, their dark eyes and large ears fixed like calendar photos. A touch of the trigger would have dropped the doe in a second.

Hesitating, I looked at the trembling fawn beneath the trees and thought of its chances of survival throughout the months ahead. As we already had one deer and the herd was small these days, I just could not destroy this animal. As I turned to walk in Grandfather's direction, the two deer trotted away quietly toward the barren.

What would Grandfather have done? Would he have allowed two deer—a winter's supply of meat—to slip from his deadly aim? I wondered. I decided this would be my little secret.

Returning to the grove, I found Grandfather nervously waiting. We walked the two-mile hike from Sandy Hill, only our voices breaking the deep silence of the woods.

As we approached the edge of our farm, the early darkness of a winter evening made the snow-covered fields seem like huge sheets spread out before us. The snow had accumulated in the settlement and was drifting across the window-lit dooryard, clinging to the old apple tree and the gables of the barn. The dog barking in the veranda was a signal to the folks inside that we were approaching.

It seemed like only minutes since we had left the house in eagerness for the day's hunt. Seeing our day together come to a close, I revealed my secret to Grandfather, a firm hunting pal, and awaited his reply.

"I saw two deer in the grove, could have shot them both," I said.

"Aah-huh," he acknowledged. "They were near the buck when I saw it first."

Then he gave me a wink as he entered the farmhouse.

38
THE WOODCUTTER
(A Short Story)

"Back up, ya black son-of-a-whore, back up," Father had shouted as he jerked on the reins, backing Prince into a place where he could hook the chain onto the gasoline engine. The old engine had been sitting just inside the open door of the shed. Prince nearly sat down; his rump was low almost to the ground and his ears were upright and alert. There was a tenseness in the animal as Father shouted and yanked on the reins. It seemed that the horse could sense the savagery in the old man's broken voice.

"Back up now," he pleaded as he lay back on the reins, putting all of his weight on the horse's bit, causing the big black stallion to twist backwards, its mouth yanked sideways, frothing.

Father hooked a chain into the ring on the engine's runners and slapped the end of the reins across the horse's rump. Prince flattened into a low pulling stance, nudging the thousand-pound engine through the shed's doorway. The engine's runners cut shallow grooves in the grassy yard on its way to the woodpile. Once the engine was in place, another trip was made to the shed for the table saw. I brought the coiled web-belt, the car battery and a tin of gasoline.

After he had put Prince back into the barn, my father moved about in the dooryard preparing to get the old engine going. His ragged grey sweater and sweat-stained felt hat blended with evening shadows so that he was almost invisible in the twilight.

"Gimme a lift here, Stevie," he shouted, grabbing one end of a huge log. Together we carried it across the yard, propping it

209

against the saw's table to help keep it steady. He had picked up the hammer to drive a nail into the end brace where a small chain would hold the table from tilting. Hurrying, he struck his thumb with the hammer, breaking the skin. In a reflex motion, he threw the hammer as hard as he could. It struck the dry shingles on the side of the woodshed with a loud crack.

"Damnation to hell," he lashed out. "The devil's here tonight."

"Call it a day. It's too dark to do anymore," I told him.

"Yah, the day's spent, I guess. Let's go in."

We walked tiredly to the farmhouse; a huge copper moon was rising above the tree-fringed horizon in the northeast, its brilliance glittering on the saw's table.

"Now, be up early," Father told me. "Be up and around when the men get here. Don't sleep all day."

Father would want to show the men that he had raised a good worker. Tomorrow, I knew, would be the test.

***

Dawn penetrated my bedroom, making the window appear a grey rectangle against a black wall. I turned, half conscious, pulling a heavy quilt of red and black patches over my shoulders, the room cold in the dull light. Downstairs, the kitchen stove snapped and cracked contentedly. A soft warmth began to filter through the doorway, making the grey September fields of frost withdraw into themselves. Muffled voices penetrated the room from the dooryard below. "Be up early, be around when the men get here": these words from last night were now fresh in my mind as I struggled into my clothing. Recognizable was George Cooper's laugh, the most hearty "Haw Haaah" in the neighbourhood, and old Charlie Moore's wheezing string of oaths.

With the occasional shout of instruction, the men were moving about the yard. The saw's flywheel was a hollow church bell bonging as the table was moved into place. The men busied themselves in the yard like beavers in the grey morning, each with the same intent, the same goal, to saw this twenty cord of maple and birch. A sense of excitement moved inside me as I gulped a breakfast; I was anxious to join them.

I went out through the front door, slipping around the

house and approaching the woodcutters from the river side. I moved into the work routine unnoticed and tried to look busy.

Some of the men were busy preparing to start the engine, others were prying the table saw into position so the belt would tract evenly on the pulleys. While the early dawn had been damp and grey, the fields and river were now tinted a deep pink by a spectacular,somehow forlorn, sunrise. There was a stiff chill that carried a ghost of winter. The men hustled around the yard, keeping themselves warm. A heavy coat of frost coloured the table saw, grey like ashes.

Old George began to crank the engine. Holding one hand over its breather, choking its throttle, he cranked the big wheels into a blurry spin, losing his hat in the scuffle.

"Choker, George, choker," someone shouted.

"Christ, she's choked to death now," snapped George.

The old engine wheezed and snorted, coughed and belched a *chunk, chunk, chunk* that made the ground jar beneath the driving piston.

"Cough, ya black son-of-a-whore, cough," said George as he stood back, the crank in his hand, watching the engine gather speed. The huge spoked wheels kicked into revolutions, the spokes becoming a grey blur as the engine sparked, gathering speed. The long belt that ran to the saw flapped in motion, almost jumping from its pulleys when the clutch was pushed in. The balance wheel and the circular saw rang its sharp jagged teeth into the morning crispness.

The men threw their coats in a heap on the ground, put on gloves, and began to hurry about, almost bumping into one another as if they were being commanded by the machine not to waste its precious working minutes and to hustle to its gait.

I took a position near the end of the table by the flywheel. Old George was working the table with Father beside him next to to the saw.

Four men carried the first log from the pile and slid it along the table as Father and George tilted it to the saw and it was laid quickly into stove-length blocks to the long whining snarls of the saw, colouring the ground yellow with its driving sawdust beneath the table and spraying my pantlegs and boot tops.

"Can ya handle 'er?" Father shouted.

"Yes sir, I can handle it okay."

"Christ yes, he can handle the job as well as any man," said old George, overhearing us. "Watch how he sets himself to throw; the boy's strong as an ox, Tom." The test had begun.

The saw snarled with ringing hunger as log after log was tilted into its rasping teeth. Sometimes the men would have to hold back on large timbers, letting the engine rebuild speed. Often they would have to turn a block completely over because of its size, sawing it from both sides. But always I kept pace, throwing blocks quickly, building the pile, proving that I could be counted on as one of the men.

The saw continued its lyrics between blocks and added the occasional ringing chime from a jagged edge. Blocks continued to press more quickly against me, bigger and heavier to handle as the morning wore on. I had to use all my energy, trying to keep poised and relaxed in the same easy fashion as the men. I continued to toss as if all eyes were watching. Beneath my flannel shirt, I trembled with exhaustion, my knees unsteady, the smell of sawdust now heavy in my clothes. I could feel the tiny particles in my boots and taste bits of wood in my teeth. When the dust at times clouded my eyes, I had to close them, throwing the blocks in darkness over my shoulders, sometimes cursing old George and the rest of the crew for this unforgivable test of manhood. And still the blocks kept coming. End on end they crowded the table in front of me, becoming an endless blur. Trembling, I continued to throw with aching arms, praying for something to break that would stop the whole operation for the day.

The pile of stove-wood grew into an oval dome beside the woodshed, and I threw block after block on top until my back and shoulders felt like numb levers extending from my inner soul, carrying the load of my own stubborn will to prove myself. I made a tier of blocks around behind me, a partition between myself and the main pile—a few less to throw. All the time the steel saw kept ringing out in uniform intervals, whining in the long snarling zings as the old engine laboured or ran easy.

For Father and the men, this day's work was more than just a job, it was a social gathering. A day when the community's men would see what kind of firewood Father had gathered, a day when Mother would serve her best dinner to be compared by the men to other meals they had had when the woodcutters were at other farms. The men would exchange little jokes, followed by a chuckle or a bark heard above the sounds of the saw. If so-and-so in the neighbourhood had a cow that was with calf or if someone was too late in getting his haying done, it all came out when the woodcutters were around. There would be gossip of perhaps someone who had to run credit at the country store or who was thought seen coming out of the widow Smith's house. The little jibing passed the day so that the work went almost unnoticed.

The pace continued. I wanted to ask Father for a break but I couldn't. I knew the men were watching and, knowing this, I struggled harder, each block a step closer to success. I felt as though I was digging myself deeper and deeper into the damp gloomy pile with its mixed scented sawdust. Occasionally, a block would roll down, gouging my ankle. I wanted to break away, run from this godawful torture, but I couldn't. I cursed silently.

Father appeared pleased with my work as he joked with old George. The men respected him. When he was with his friends he would suddenly become one of them. Then there was no compassion, no weakness. But it seemed when he and I were alone he was a different person, a kind, sensitive man who never drove himself or anyone else. Maybe his manhood was being tested here, too. I would have to hold up my end of the job for both of our sakes.

It was like when Father and I were in church and I would sing along with him because we were sharing a hymn book and he was singing. I would follow along in support, the two of us together in the back of the church, the only ones there singing. It was like we were singing now, only the rest of the crew couldn't hear us. There was something inside each of us that blended into a deep harmony that only we could feel. I would exhaust myself to help him prove a point to his friends but, for my part, I wasn't sure if the point was worth proving or if it meant anything at all to me. It was more for his sake that I laboured. Father smiled faintly.

My undershirt, now soaking with sweat, glued itself to my back and chest. The hair beneath my cap was also wet and sticky and my head was itching, the beads of sweat stinging in my eyes, blurring my vision. Once in a while the sweat would drop from my nose and run sweet in my mouth so that I was able to taste my own soul pouring out in agony. There seemed no end; yet I could now at least understand the day's full purpose.

And then, as if the old engine knew something the men themselves didn't, it suddenly quit sparking and coasted to a gentle downhill stop.

"She's outta gas," Father shouted. "Let's all take a break, boys."

The men sat on blocks in the lee of the woodpile where the sun was warm and they lighted cigarettes, rolling their own by hand from a pouch of loose tobacco passed around. The scent of tobacco smoke, human sweat, sawdust and gasoline blended into a sweet perfume that drifted past me. I craved a cigarette myself but thought better of it in Father's presence.

When the men had finished smoking, Father cranked the engine and the saw was ringing again. This time one of the other men took over at the table where I had spent the morning. I was moved to the other side of the yard where I could help carry to the saw. The afternoon slipped past and soon the pile was finished and the woodcutters were gone. Our dooryard was a mountain range of maple blocks.

The yellow September day had already begun to fade into a damp charcoal evening. Father and I went for a long walk down by the river. A Canada jay hopped before us on the pathway, screaming as it was spooked into flight. The sounds of the driving engine and the ringing saw were still echoing faintly in my ears. We stood watching the broad river. Father said, "Would you like a cigarette, Steve?"